RAVE REVIEWS FOR KEEP ON MOVING

"KEEP ON MOVING is one man's transparent, honest reflections on the journey that has given him the courage to take his final steps with joy and to keep exploring and growing. It is important that this is a man's story and a black man at that. His willingness to expose his vulnerabilities, fears, and joys to openly and fully share himself is refreshing. It is a lesson for all but especially men, that it's not our life circumstances that define who we are but how we choose to respond to those circumstances. Ron has constantly chosen to love, believe, grow, and share what he has learned with others. And, in his 4th quarter, he continues to do the same."

-Marilyn Chase, Former Assistant Secretary Commonwealth of
Massachusetts, Executive Office Health and Human Services

"Wow! The book was filled with so much wisdom and sage advice. It was such a transparent reflection of you, your family, passions, concerns, hopes, and aspirations. I will forever cherish the phrase "keep on moving" with new meaning and appreciation for the clarity of your example, "living with the present while reflecting on the past and bringing it all together. The journal entries (and photos) were an added window into your soul and an affirmation of a life well-lived. More than anything, I was moved by the book to rethink some things in my own life (especially as I reflect on the 4th Quarter). BTW—I love the metaphor...

-Alan J. Ingram, Ed.D. - Ingram Consulting, LLC

"At the peak of his life, Ron Ancrum developed a debilitating medical condition. When his illness worsened, he started a journal that eventually evolved into a memoir. He reveals his warm, loving bond with his mother, his strained relationship with his father, and the nurturing influence of his grandparents.

Throughout this book, he stresses; the need to contribute to society, show kindness to family, friends, and community, set principles and values to guide your actions, and function with the highest level of integrity. This book may serve as a guide for anyone planning to retire and offers suggestions that one might use should they have a debilitating illness.

As you approach the end of this beautiful story about Ron and his loving wife and family, you are likely to wish for triple overtime."

-Dr. Harris Gibson, Jr., Professor of Thoracic Surgery,
Boston University

KEEP ON MOVING

Mynd Matters Publishing
715 Peachtree Street NE
Suites 100 & 200
Atlanta, GA 30308

e-ISBN: 978-1-953307-81-1
ISBN: 978-1-953307-79-8 (pbk)
ISBN: 978-1-953307-80-4 (hdcv)

KEEP ON MOVING

MY JOURNEY IN THE FOURTH QUARTER

RON ANCRUM

To my wife, Pamela Cross Ancrum,
Writing these words and enjoying life for so many years
would not be possible without you.

Contents

The Four Quarters of Life

IT'S BETTER TO LIVE LIFE WITH A SPIRITED SOUL AND A HOPEFUL HEART.

A few years ago, I developed the fundamental principle that life has four quarters. Like football or basketball, as the time clock elapses, things get more intense or heightened, and you find yourself playing catch-up or trying to hold on to whatever advantages you gained in the first three quarters. For example, most of us try to stay young by using cosmetics or acting young at heart. Most men shave their beards to keep the gray hairs from showing. I let the gray hairs come in because others have told me how distinguished it appeared. Now my head is bald, and my goatee is white. Forget about the physical self. You inevitably change your body shape. Gaining weight, especially a gut, was not in my plans. You look at yourself and wonder how you got here. I paid close attention to what I was eating, and periodically, I would exercise. Obviously, the exercise was insufficient, and I could not do without my ice cream dish at night.

As you get older and up in age, you start to forget things that just happened yesterday. Where are my keys? Where did I put that piece of paper? It becomes harder to remember faces or places. But unlike a sporting competition, you neither know where you're heading nor the time when life will end, so you keep moving forward for as long as you are able. A game clock will run out of time and has an expected finite end. If there's anything I have learned, it's better to live life with a spirited soul and a hopeful heart. Don't worry about time. Things have a way of working themselves out. Don't let all the negative happenings around you destroy your demeanor. And always give favor to your faith in God and family.

So, how do I define the four quarters? From birth through approximately age twenty, the first quarter is the development period. You graduate from high school and start down one of the many paths to choose something. The path might be college, which was my choice, or entering the workforce. This period is when we learn the most. We develop our personality and determine what we like and dislike. But that may change over time as we constantly experience new things. Most of us have very little responsibility at this stage. Still, before the quarter is over, you will hopefully begin to realize that you are responsible for yourself and your destiny. For me, those college years were great. I never returned home to Stamford, Connecticut to live.

The second quarter takes us to age forty-two, when we are probably the most productive. I remember having the most energy during those years, and my professional life began to rise. I was active and could do just about anything I wanted. As I did at age twenty-six, some get married and start a family during this quarter. Raising children becomes a primary focus. At work, you begin to position yourself to climb the corporate ladder, or you still don't know what you want to do with the rest of your life and keep searching for it. Having an active social life is paramount, so you gravitate towards many personal connections. You establish new friends, acquaintances, or colleagues with similar and sometimes varying interests. It's probably your moment of experimentation.

The third quarter will bring you to age sixty-five, when you begin to settle down. You mature, hopefully gracefully, gain wisdom to share with younger adults, and, whether you like it or not, begin to experience aging. You become more resistant to change and prefer to keep life simple. I began to have fewer concerns about my career because I had already established myself to my satisfaction. I was more focused on the other things I wanted to do in my life that I currently did not have time to do. For some of us, we at least start thinking about whether we can retire and how soon we would like to retire. If you have children, they are now adults, and you find out your parenting job is not over. You receive recognition for your work, talent, contributions, and achievements.

As I write this, it's without question; I am now in the **FOURTH QUARTER!** I had initially planned to retire around age sixty-two, and then it got pushed back to age sixty-five. It wasn't until I turned sixty-eight years old that I officially retired. I feel my age every day. I physically feel it, and my health issues are more pronounced than ever before. As someone said to me, "When you wake up in the morning and the pain you feel is not a new one, it's a good day." But more importantly, I have learned how to be more patient. There's absolutely no reason for me to rush or expect immediate satisfaction. No need to get upset or stressed. I have a saying that goes, "If I accomplish at least one thing each day, I will have done 365 things in a year." I no longer have to do things I don't choose to do. As a gift, my wife gave me a t-shirt with the phrase, "I don't want to, I don't have to, you can't make me, I'm retired." This mantra is my new attitude, and it can only manifest itself in the Fourth Quarter. I try to be both carefree and careful at the same time. I minimize activities that are stressful and cause anxiety. At the same time, there are some things I should not do to stay safe from harm.

For *Keep On Moving*, my story begins at age sixty with a birthday celebration for which I spent more than a year planning. I got excited about birthday milestones and wanted to do something similar to what I'd done for my 50th birthday. The party had 125 of my friends, family, and guests at the premier Sculler's Jazz Club in Boston. The headliner, Panamanian pianist Danilo Perez and other musician friends, performed.

This time, ten years later, we held the party at an area restaurant, X&O, owned by our neighbor. We asked people to donate money to benefit the Mattapan Community Health Center, an agency my wife and I supported for many years. Entertainment included a recognized local R&B award-winning singer. She was a former neighbor of ours when we lived in Dorchester and later, a professional colleague of mine. Another friend, the founder of the annual Boston Women of Color Comedy Show, kicked off the event with some standup comedy. She is an unexpectedly funny person whose humor was well-suited for the mixed crowd of adults. There was also a

DJ for a bit of dancing and several billiard tables for nine-ball.

This time, we had ninety-one guests (according to the guest book), family members, church family, friends, and colleagues. I'm not sure how much we raised that day, but the agency director appreciated the gift. I was delighted to have my special day and, at the same time, do some charitable work. My upcoming milestones will be to celebrate my 75th birthday (2024) and 50 years of marriage (2026).

Since that birthday, I have held two more jobs, and moved from Boston, with its long cold winters, to the gracious southern hospitality of the *Queen City*, Charlotte, North Carolina. Around this time, my health started to become the focal point, and life took a slight turn. November 2018 is when I began writing in a journal. It was the day immediately following my return home from being in the hospital. I don't write in the journal every day, only when I feel there's something on my mind to share. I started to do this initially to track my health, mainly to document how I was feeling and the changes we would make regarding treatment. I use it to express my thoughts on everything: activities, opinions on world issues, and my random take on life. My goal was to reflect on what's going on around me and in the world. The journal includes various aspects of life during the Fourth Quarter while living with an incurable disease and being retired. It was a method for me to reflect on the past and the present. The journal provides a way to share my life's journey and lessons learned along the way.

After two years, I decided to take my journal entries, seventy-seven of them, and write this book, which was not the initial purpose. So, why a book? Because I have more to share than a simple essay or journal release. Memoirs are typically written by celebrity types, of which I am not. While I have accomplished quite a bit, I am not a superstar. Within my professional world and the community, I achieved a level of recognition but still not above the best in the field. Together with my wife Pam, we were able to carve out a very comfortable lifestyle, yet we are far from wealthy. My thoughts may not be profound, but they have just enough wisdom to pass along to another person, a peer, or a mentee.

A lot has happened during the last decade. Life has been usual to some degree, yet the journey has taken an unexpected turn. The book covers various aspects of living in the Fourth Quarter. However, the journey can be longer than I anticipated, so I must keep moving forward.

CHAPTER 1

Family

WHEN FAMILY MEMBERS STAY IN TOUCH, GATHER AT HOLIDAYS, AND PROVIDE SUPPORT WHEN NEEDED, THE MOST IMPORTANT THING IS TO REMEMBER THE LOVE OF FAMILY IS ESSENTIAL.

To understand how I think about the world or myself at this stage of my life, you need to know about my upbringing, the family I was born into, and the family I've created. When it comes to family, I'm not sure how *typical* we are, but it is what it is.

My mother, Clifford, now lives in Maryland. She was born in New York City but lived in several states, including Virginia and Illinois, and later moved to Stamford, Connecticut, where she completed high school and married my dad, Vernon.

When I was nine years old, they got a divorce. My dad had just returned home after several years in prison. Everyone who ever knew my dad agrees he was always angry, drank too much, and would get into fights. I grew up in fear of this man and worried about what he might do to us in a fit of rage spurred by alcohol. We moved to New York City (Bronx) to get away from him. By the end of that summer, I cried to return to live with my grandparents, Virginia and Winson Ancrum, which my mother permitted, thank goodness. However, it meant my father was around, but I was not under his custody.

I had often said that my paternal grandparents raised me to my mother's dislike. Mom kept in touch, communicated often, and would send money to help support my needs. However, I remember most of my childhood living in the Ancrum household. We lived on Rose Park in Stamford and later

moved to a house they purchased on West Avenue. As a child, I always had a home, food on the table, clothes on my back and plenty of love. But in the house, with as many as six people living there, we had one bathroom, no shower, and as a teenager, I slept in the dining room on a small bed with a desk nearby. My clothes hung in a closet in the hallway. Yet, I survived just fine and actually lived with my grandparents through my first year of college.

Like many Black families, my grandparents migrated north from Orangeburg, South Carolina, in the '30s. My grandfather was not a well-educated man. He worked at a sheet metal factory which you could see in his hands. He tended a garden at home, wore suspenders, and dressed up for church where he was a deacon. Overall, he was a gentle man. However, my dad always had a way to get his father annoyed, and they would fight, sometimes physically. I enjoyed having breakfast with Grandad, eating grits with sardines, and drinking Postum, a powdered roasted grain coffee substitute. He loved rice so much that he ate it with every dinner. He always had Life Savers® mints on him, too. During my school years, he was my barber. Not a fun experience. He would hold your head in his hand and take that razor and just cut it all off. No styling, no edging, just a cut.

My grandmother was such a loving and caring person. Everyone gravitated towards her for her kindness. She provided whatever I needed in addition to what I received from my mother. And the food she cooked, especially during holidays, was great southern cooking. She loved canning food. The fruits, in particular, were my favorites—peaches, pears, apples, and blueberries. When I was in college, I would bring her a basket of apples to preserve.

You often hear about the statistics of young Black men growing up with single parents or with grandparents. Sometimes, in the right circumstances, those young Black men can succeed. You learn the difference between good and evil and then decide how you'll behave. It is essential not to let the negative tendencies influence you to do wrong.

The other male figure in my life was my Uncle Donnie. Our relationship was special. As an adult, I realized he was my surrogate father and big brother rolled into one. If not for him, I would not be who I am. In 2017, he passed away. I had many more tears for him than I did for my birth father when he died. I wished Uncle Donnie had come to live with us in Massachusetts after Beverly (his love) passed away in 2015. Before he transitioned, we had time to talk, and I expressed

how much I appreciated all he had done for me. The last time we spoke, he was in the hospital. Uncle Donnie said he was feeling much better and would be coming home soon. Two days later, he died. That's when I realized he was talking about going up to heaven.

Uncle Donnie had a great smile and was the kindest guy you want to know. He had a way of making quick friends with the people who waited tables at his favorite places to eat or at the store where he picked up his daily newspaper. They all loved him.

My wife, Pam, is an amazing person and God's gift to me. Sometimes a little old-fashioned, but beautiful inside and out. She may never know how much I love her because it's not my nature to express myself that way, but I can't imagine my life without her. We have found a way to persevere through the various jobs that took me away from home. I worked in upstate New York at Colgate when we lived in Hartford. I traveled extensively around the country when we lived in Dorchester, Massachusetts, because of the consulting business. I worked in Springfield, Massachusetts (the western part of the state), at the community foundation when we lived in Canton, Massachusetts (the eastern part of the state), and then finally worked at Boston College after moving to Charlotte, constantly commuting a long distance between work and home. Maybe she relished me being away so I would not annoy her with my silly behavior.

My wife and I talk all the time about how blessed we have been. We have been married for almost forty-five years and continue to enjoy our life together. We moved to Charlotte, five years ago and have found a few other folks we already knew who moved from Connecticut and Massachusetts and many new friends that we socialize with on a fairly regular basis. We can travel a lot more now because we have the time.

When people ask me about our relationship, I tell them we never fight. It does not mean we always agree, but we can discuss things without an argument. Marriage also requires sacrifice, a willingness to support the other person even if you might not think it's the right decision. Without question, you need to work hard on building a solid marriage, and we can do this, at least I think so. As you read this book, I'll have more to say about Pam and our relationship.

The second female in our immediate household is Erica, our daughter. Like most parents, you enjoy watching your beautiful daughter grow into the person she will become as an adult. As a parent, I was not a very good tooth fairy—she caught me. I fell asleep while reading a book at bedtime. But the best support I gave her was showing up at her sports events. She has more talent than she gives herself credit for. In my opinion, her photography is superb as she has an eye for taking photos, capturing just the right subject, light, location, and distance. I wish she would make photography a significant part of her life but her journey through life will be wherever it goes and whatever she decides. Erica is highly organized, very detail-oriented, and does not procrastinate, all good attributes. We provide some help and offer more advice than she might want, but we're her parents. These days, I hope to share as much with her on how to move beyond her Second Quarter. Now that she's an adult, she listens more to what I have to say.

Our immediate family is small. Even though I grew up as an only child, after my mother got remarried, I gained a sister, LaMonde. She's much younger than me, so we never lived in the same household but our relationship has grown closer over the years. I can remember her as a little girl, but we started to really connect when it was time for her to go to college. I took her on a trip to visit a few schools, trying to help her make the right decision. She attended and graduated from Hampton University, which I thought was an excellent choice.

I have many cousins I stay in touch with from my father's and mother's families. Some are around my age, like Joe French and Marlene Harris. But the family is spread across the U.S., from Connecticut to California. The most precious moments have always been Thanksgiving and Christmas holidays. These are no longer big family gatherings, instead only a few of us get together. Regardless, the highlight of the day is still dinner, which includes plenty of our favorite foods.

From My Journal:

<u>November 25, 2018</u> — *Today is the Sunday after Thanksgiving. Family members, Mom and Erica, arrived on the Tuesday before the holiday. We typically spend the holiday with family members but this year was small. It's just the six of us including Phyllis (Pam's sister), and a friend, Sandra.*

We have had some interesting conversations. My mother makes some comment that usually shows her age or a perspective, then one of us challenges that notion. Phyllis will make a comment that reflects her thoughts, and we react to that. We don't argue, but we think differently on some topics. The biggest issue is trying to find something on TV to watch, which is nearly impossible. The parade worked in the morning then I got a couple of hours of football. Unfortunately, there is no movie or program without violence or sex. Most comedy programs are okay.

By the time we ate, it got better. Food is a way for us to come together. Of course, Pam cooked all day and there are tons of leftovers we will still be eating later today for dinner. This year, I believe my Mom and Phyllis enjoyed each other's company more than ever. When we got a break, I took some time to interview my mom and we talked about her life from childhood to now.

This trip will probably be Mom's last to Charlotte. She walks, leaning to one side, a little hunched over. She says her hips and her feet bother her, so she cannot stand up straight. I have to encourage her to use her cane. Her memory is okay, but she forgets things now and then.

It's early <u>Christmas morning, 2018</u>, and I'm the only one up at 7:30 AM. Pam is kind of awake, but I'm sure tired after waiting up for Phyllis to come in from singing at her church's Christmas Eve service. Phyllis spent the night here, so she's with us this morning. Erica is sleeping. She never wants to rise early, but she'll get up when everyone else does. We have spent holidays, probably the last four decades, with just the four of us. We try to keep it small, meaning, not too many gifts, but the tree has many wrapped boxes, envelopes on the tree, and stockings stuffed with items. We always have breakfast first, grab a coffee or other beverage, and then unwrap the gifts. I usually put on some Christmas music; maybe I'll let Alexa do the honor.

I'm planning to have basketball on TV this year. There are five games to watch, all worth seeing. The C's play at 5:30 PM. I hope to get us playing games, Uno® or Scrabble®, or something to have fun. We will not go out anywhere or visit any friends or family nearby. It's just us.

If I have not said it before, I have been blessed with an enriched life. I'm still able to help others and move forward.

We rarely get to see our family members. Some years, we drive to Maryland for Thanksgiving to visit with my mother and sister. But for the past two years, that was not the case. Also, we decided my mother was not strong enough to endure air travel, a train, or a long car ride. Since she will not be coming to visit us, it means driving to her.

We made a few trips to Maryland to start the process for her eventual move into assisted living. My mother was a little hesitant to make the change, so I had to convince her it was necessary. She set her target date for April 2020. I, more than anyone, wanted her to make the shift so she could receive daily home care services while still being independent.

Pam's sister, Phyllis, had moved to Charlotte and lived in a lovely apartment only ten minutes from our house. Calvin, Pam's brother, passed in 2018, and his three daughters live too far away to visit by car. We all make telephone calls to wish one another a happy holiday, but nothing compares to having family gather in person for food, music, laughter, reminiscing, and, of course, more food. Phone calls, text messages, and emails are okay, but not the same. When the entire family cannot be there, we have found enjoyment in inviting a few other friends who would otherwise be alone.

From My Journal:

Thanksgiving 2019 (12/3/19) – _We did not travel to Maryland to be with family (LaMonde, Chris and Danielle, Nicole, Mom, and Kevin). Instead, last Thursday, we stayed in Charlotte for Thanksgiving and had our usual big dinner. This year, Erica and Phyllis represented her family. We invited four other people including, John and Valerie Caldwell, who moved here from Boston and attended Charles Street AME_ *church, they bought a home here before we did but fully moved in last month. The other two guests were friends from Pam's book club. Sandra joined us last year, and Rosebud from Pam's book club has lots of stories and a very positive personality.*

We had lots of food, and everyone came prepared to load up their Tupperware after. Leftovers lasted until Sunday's dinner. This is one of those holidays that you have fond family memories of large gatherings. All hands-on deck in the kitchen, lots of noise because everyone is talking, the TV on football, or some other show that few are watching. But those days don't exist for us anymore. In general, until our guests arrived, it was a tranquil day. I watched a little football but mainly had music playing.

Today's celebration should be much more focused on being thankful. Sometimes we take for granted all that we have, the material things. It's a time to embrace family and friends who might need a hug or words to demonstrate your support. It's a time to take a day off from being critical, expressing hate, or committing an act of violence. And yet, in some households across this country, people were shot over an argument, people showed their anger, and we all have something negative to say about someone else. So, just praise God and show your love.

Christmas Time (12-27-19) – *It's two days after Christmas, early in the morning. Erica has been visiting for a week and is heading back to Boston today. This year felt very different. Some of our traditions were modified to adjust to our various life changes. We always open gifts after breakfast with a cup of coffee and music but with Phyllis not staying at the house, we did not pick her up until later which meant opening gifts around noon.*

Leading up to today, most of my shopping has been online. No more trips to the mall, going store to store. I did hit Macy's one day, but that was it. No more day post-Christmas shopping at the mall; much better than heading to crowded stores. Instead, I used the time to think about who to talk to—call or by text message— to wish them a Merry Christmas or Happy New Year. As usual, we spoke to the family. My family made it easy. They were all at LaMonde's in the afternoon. Mom, Chris, Dani and Naomi Brielle (the new baby), and Nicole. Naomi was born on December 8, and we got to visit them on December 13. A lovely and beautiful baby girl.

This week, Erica and I spent time talking about her life and plans. She should move from her apartment this summer because the rent keeps going higher. She needs a new job; her salary is not increasing. She prefers to stay in Boston but is considering moving to NC to be closer to us. Finding work in Charlotte will be difficult, so her job search needs to be broad. Pray for her!

My mom celebrated her 90th birthday in April 2021. She keeps active and loves to talk and laugh. She is very particular about her clothes and hair and enjoys Bible study. In October 2020, I finished a book for Mom titled, *We Call her Clifford:*

From Son to Mother. The book was a great accomplishment for me because I do not see myself as a writer and feel more comfortable with numbers. Mom was pleasantly surprised and pleased with the book that tells her story. My goal was not about mainstream sales or distribution so I only sent copies of the book to family members.

As you enter the Fourth Quarter, you begin to understand the importance of family, if it hadn't already crossed your mind. As a child growing up, you develop under the watchful care of family members. By observing, you learn that family members take care of each other when things get tough. Despite all the strife my dad gave my grandparents, they always let him back into the home. Some family members would have kicked him out and told him never to return. Also, I watched how my grandmother took care of children from other families when their guardians were in need. My uncle took care of her when she got older and everyone else in the family, including his siblings, Vernon and Dorothy. When it was my turn, I did not hesitate to do whatever I could for Uncle Donnie. When Erica was only five, I said to her repeatedly, "I take care of you now, and you take care of me later." Although caring is an important attribute to discover from within yourself, for some family members, it might be asking too much.

You begin to separate yourself from your family as you enter the 2nd and 3rd quarters of life. You are developing into your professional career, hopefully starting and supporting your own family. But when your kids are grown, they need to understand you might depend on them for help and support as you become elderly. Somehow God will provide.

So, why is my family not closer? We don't fight or argue over things and appear to get along when we're together. Maybe we just never grasped the culture of our ancestors. As a child, our families always got together during the holidays (all of them). That tradition has faded away. Over the past few years, I tried to see my mother every Thanksgiving. Either she visits us, or we go to my sister's house. After losing her husband and son, Pam's sister, Phyllis, always spent Christmas with us. We wanted to make sure she was not alone. We convinced her to move to Charlotte near us, and we saw her just about every day. These are special moments not to take for granted.

The family from l to r top: Pam, Erica, Nicole, Danielle, Chris;
bottom: Ron, Mom, Naomi, LaMonde (2020)

When family members stay in touch, gather on holidays, and provide support when needed, the most important thing is to remember that love is essential. Mom and I now use a fabulous device called GrandPad. She can talk to me using video to receive text messages and email, receive and view photos, and listen to music. During the pandemic, we could not just drive up there to visit. This device made it possible to connect visually.

CHAPTER 2

Friends

Throughout your life, you will have many, many friends. Some for life and others are just passing through. Most people you know are simply acquaintances or colleagues. They are there for that moment in time, and then they fade away. Not because you wanted that to happen. You probably could have done something to stay in contact, but neither party took that step. Just count the number of "friends" you still have from your hometown. Each time you move, you start over again to make new friends. Do you still keep in touch with them? How about the bridesmaids and groomsmen at your wedding? For me, these were all crucial relationships that helped define who I am and to tell my story.

My lifelong friend is (William) Bruce Monroe. We have known each other as school pals, and our friendship endures today. We did everything together while attending schools in Stamford. He was the brother I never had. He calls my mother, Mom, and I did the same with his. I would do anything he asked of me, and I know I can count on him. For the most part, we were very much alike growing up, especially in terms of being musicians. Our family backgrounds are similar and we joke that our fathers attended the same college, which was imprisonment. We celebrate each other's wedding anniversaries and birthdays, except Bruce is much better at remembering dates than me.

On two occasions, we recently got together at our high school's 50th graduation celebration in 2017. If you've ever been to a high school reunion, identifying some of your classmates is a problem because they can look so different. Of course, you think you still look good. In 2019, I had an opportunity to stop by to visit him and his wife, Mary, at home in Florida. We got to share how we were doing, tell new stories, and have a good time laughing about life.

Ours is the most precious and valuable relationship you can have, especially for a Black man. You can rarely talk to someone about anything and know they got your back. Even though we do not see each other often, Bruce is just a call or text message away. It's also refreshing we are not exactly alike and do different things now that we are older. Bruce does not attend church, but I know he believes in God. His religion is spending time on the golf course, which he does a few times per week. Even though I don't play golf and we don't belong to the same clubs, we enjoy our respective groups and have similar interest in music and sports. Bruce is a special person in my life, without question.

Then there's my spiritual brother, Alan Ingram, my buddy from Oklahoma City. Our relationship does not center around the church, but he and I have a special bond because of our commonalities. We met in 2009 when we were working in Springfield, Massachusetts. We were both in the city in very prestigious and visible leadership positions. We were hesitant to move our families there, which our respective employers did not like. We dealt with very conservative people who fought against everything we wanted to do. We shared a love of sports, jazz, and dining out with wine. We grew up with similar backgrounds. Ours is a relationship meant to be. When we both left those jobs, he found work in Boston that allowed us to continue our friendship. After serving in the Air Force and working in Education, Alan is now semi-retired. He consults and travels extensively around the country. Most of the time, one of us will send a text message to the other to keep in contact, share what's going on, and praise God for all that he has done for us. What we have will be a long-lasting relationship.

Along one's professional journey, you pick up a "partner in crime." In the 1980s, that was Frank Williams. He worked at the regional office of The College Board. We spent time together, attempting to address the issues we faced as Black men in the higher education college admissions and financial aid fields. Along with a few other colleagues, we worked to bring greater diversity to the profession and service in the associations. That relationship grew into a more personal friendship. We were in an investment club together, learning how to buy stocks—unfortunately, not very well. We played tennis at Sportsmen's Tennis Club, a Black-owned center in Boston. We hung out with two other men, Rudy and Donald, to shoot the breeze as brothers can do from time to time. This kind of relationship can withstand years apart, never die, and pick up where we left off. That's a special bond.

In Charlotte, Pam and I have developed some new friends. Pam has her book club, and I have the Charlotte Jazz Buzz (CJB), a group of Black men who enjoy listening to jazz. I transferred my Boule membership from Springfield and Boston to Charlotte. We now have a church home, Friendship Missionary Baptist Church, and we have started to develop new relationships there, as we had at Charles Street AME in Boston. We joined a group of twelve couples to form the Onyx Wine Club that met bi-monthly until the pandemic paused the face-to-face gatherings. When meeting, we would bring wines to taste and enjoy with dinner. We enjoyed this creative and entrepreneurial group of professionals representing different generations.

The transition to Charlotte was easier because we already knew a few folks that had moved from Boston, such as Pam and Willie Jones, John and Valerie Caldwell, Juanita and Ken Wade, Natalie and Michael McIver. There are other friends from Connecticut, like Adrianne and Lenzy Wallace, in Charlotte. We were also introduced to Linda and Bob Keene through our mutual friends up north. More recently, Lee and Sheila Shephard relocated from Boston as well. We are now socially busier than we have ever been before.

All of our new friends in Charlotte result from engaging in various social networks. Although the term social network refers to the internet, in this circumstance, the wine club, fraternity, and men's clubs are how I define these groups. Like me, the people in these groups moved here from the Northeast or Midwest and retired. All of these interactions keep me engaged and active.

I learned from a discussion with one of my new friends that all my social networks are with Black folks. It made me realize I was unintentionally engaged in activities whereby having new white friends in Charlotte has not happened. I grew up in an integrated environment, school, neighborhood, and work. I've always had white friends from childhood to adulthood through work or professional associations and musicians. It's not as if Charlotte is without white people. There are plenty here. Most of them I come across are incredible people that support similar social causes. Of course, you might see a Confederate flag on the front porch if you take a drive outside the county. It's not because I decided to segregate myself or adopt an absolute pro-

Black posture. Like most people, I find myself socializing with others like myself. I could and probably should seek other opportunities that are more diverse. It has made me think about who my white friends are today. Am I keeping in touch with the friends from my past, or will these relationships fade away over time because I'm no longer in their daily lives? Some of these relationships go back as far as fourth grade. A few are former work colleagues and social activists in Boston that I keep in contact with and will continue to do so. I believe it's essential to interact in a diverse circle to enable open and emotionally complex conversations about race. I can do better here in Charlotte. I will.

Keeping in touch with current and past friends is not the easiest thing. During the Fourth Quarter, you begin to think about those precious moments and wonder how certain person are doing, where they are, and whether or not they work full-time or are retired. Sometimes, you wonder if they are still alive or deceased, and if you were unaware. There are others with who I keep in contact from my hometown, college years, workplaces, professional associations, and the community. Thank goodness for Facebook and LinkedIn, which make it possible to locate, connect, and send brief messages to acknowledge what they are doing and for you to share your actions. I rarely post photos or comments on these social media platforms, but these tools help to reach out to people from my past.

In November 2018, I sent the following message to friends on Facebook:

From My Journal:

Last year, I was in the hospital because I was having severe breathing issues. This past week, Pam told most of you I was under the weather again. My breathing issues came back, but I did not want to spend any time staying in the hospital, so I hunkered down for one week with my personal care attendant, Pam, under the doctor's orders, and fought to get back to my usual. Thank God I am beginning to feel better. We went out this morning to the pharmacy and BJ's. This may not sound very exciting, but getting out of the house is a good thing. It provides me an opportunity to get some fresh air and exercise.

I'm hoping to enjoy this weekend but I need to be mindful of not doing too much. Activity is good for the body and mind, but too much activity is harmful to the lungs and heart. I'm now on a higher dosage of meds (ugh) and an increased oxygen level. You'll probably see me with an extra bag of batteries and chargers just to ensure I have enough power for the portable device. The following two weeks are particularly busy with many meetings and events, followed by the holidays when our daughter Erica will visit.

I'm sharing this information with you because I want you to know what's going on. More importantly, I might need your help. Maybe my message can help you or somebody else you know. Too often, people keep so much inside and private that we keep the ones closest to us in the dark. This is for you, not the general public.

I want all of you to give Pam much love for all she does to take care of me as well as her sister, Phyllis. Caring for me must be an extreme burden on her, but she would never let you know or show any signs of stress. On Sunday, say a prayer for us, not for God's healing but His strength. Pam and I have been blessed in so many ways, and I have so much to be thankful for. I need to be stronger. We love our new city and have been embraced by so many loving friends. [sic]

To God be the Glory, Ron

I expected some "thumb up likes" or short comments, but a few friends expressed more than that. Here are a few:

Hi Ron-

. . . just reading your message and have tears flowing at the same time. Yes, I read the part in your message about reading with a celebration...but I can't help it as this was unexpected. I knew you were experiencing a health issue a while ago, and I guess I assumed it was being addressed and not severe. Do realize that I've only known and seen you be the caregiver and not the one in need of care over the years. So, I need a moment to adjust and possibly reflect here. Not from the point of sadness, but a place of brotherhood, friendship, love, and respect.

From the beginning of my introduction to Charles Street and the CSAME family, you have been such a source of encouragement...not only to me but to others. I've admired and continue to respect you and appreciate being a part of both your circle and extended family. some of my most treasured memories have been with you and Pam (vacation trip, focus group, Celtic games, dinners, and fundraisers). I say this simply to say that I love you and am here for you as well as Pam. Anything we can do, just ask. You both have been a special blessing to us, and I wish we could be there for you during those difficult times. [sic] – TC

❋ ❋ ❋

Thanks, Ron, for sharing your journal entry in the email below. Know that you all continue to be in our prayers (for strength). I can't tell you how much the gift of your friendship (kinship) means to me, and I thank God we connected while in Springfield. Commuting, for me, had its inherent challenges. Lisa and I owe you and Pam a great debt to welcome me to Boston and include me in your outings. Some of my fondest memories of Boston are from the times we shared in fellowship (e.g., exceptional sporting events, good food/restaurants, rich conversations, great jazz, and spirit-filled worship services).

My friends and extended family circle are relatively small by choice but special and important. You (and Pam) are definitely a part of it.

I'm reminded of one of my favorite scriptures in Philippians 4:13 "I can do all things through Christ, who gives me strength." Know that you are not alone in your health challenges. I'm sure you have a support system in place, but please don't hesitate to let me know if I can do anything to help or lend a hand with. - AI

❀ ❀ ❀

Ron,

There is a lot I would like to say, but I will say what is necessary. You and Pam are not alone. Monica and I are in your lives for a reason.

Please know that you have our thoughts and prayers, but you also have our commitment to being there for you and Pam, no matter what! We are available to help when and where ever needed.

That includes helping you and Pam with daily activities, chores around the house, changing a light bulb, running an errand, fixing something, driving you somewhere, picking up something, whatever is needed; I hope you get the message! We are here to help.

If you and Pam need someone to talk to, we are good listeners.

Thoughts and prayers are good, but all hands-on-deck is also needed. [sic] - EB & MD

❀ ❀ ❀

These are examples of what friends do when they are asked to respond. They begin with words of encouragement and provide the necessary empathy, not sympathy, to let you know they hear you and understand. I can only hope I do the same when my friends reach out to me. These relationships are critical for not feeling alone. They can help you retain your sanity and keep you from depression.

We did not think about how many friends we were leaving behind in Boston. We just assumed we would maintain our connection, and we would see them during our visits to Boston or they would visit us here. A group of our dearest friends in Boston (the New Year's Eve Crew) is still in touch, but we cannot see them much. Since moving South, we were able to get together with the Sidberry's when they traveled to North Carolina. We had celebrated New Year's Eve together for more than thirty years. We took a group vacation a few times and celebrated each other's accomplishments. When we started, none of us had children, and now the kids are all adults forging their careers. December 31, 2020, we did a Zoom NYE gathering. What fun!

During the Fourth Quarter, you start to lose old friends due to distance apart, illness, and death. I suspect that while our circle is large now, it will shrink over time. In the meantime, I can be thankful for these relationships and play my part.

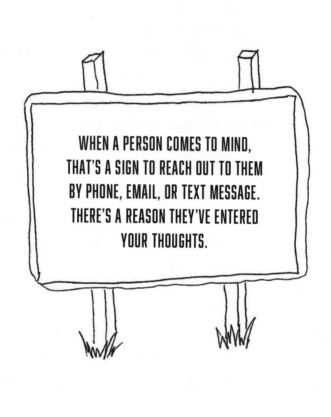

WHEN A PERSON COMES TO MIND, THAT'S A SIGN TO REACH OUT TO THEM BY PHONE, EMAIL, OR TEXT MESSAGE. THERE'S A REASON THEY'VE ENTERED YOUR THOUGHTS.

CHAPTER 3

Retirement

PLANNING FOR RETIREMENT IS CRITICAL. THERE IS NOT A RIGHT TIME TO MAKE
THIS CHANGE. YOU MUST WANT IT AND NOT FEEL IT'S BEING FORCED ON YOU.

As I said earlier, based on my theory, I entered the Fourth Quarter at the end of 2015. I resigned from my position at Nurtury Learning Lab, and we moved to Charlotte. That job was a significant departure from all my other work. In the heart of the community, I was on the ground, interacting directly with the children and families. It was not your typical facility we were building but rather a state-of-the-art program. I was very proud to be the director of an early childhood education center located in Boston's most prominent public housing development.

I could dwell on the accomplishments of building a $17 million early education school, but that was not the personal gain from my new experience. Yes, the Bromley Heath Center children, located in the basement of a public housing building, were moved into the state's most impressive early education facility. As the director, hiring the staff, developing the programs, and helping to raise money were my more significant responsibilities.

The three years as director offer time to learn more about myself and the people we served, many of them in poverty, as its defined. I learned more about early childhood education and its importance to physical and mental development. I now understand that families in public housing do not choose to be in their situation, but our system puts them there and keeps most of them there for decades, if not generations. Many of the parents I met worked hard to provide for their children.

As a school, we were open to organized events and activities for the whole community and not just the families with children in attendance. We locked the doors for safety reasons but opened the doors so the Bromley-Heath families could also enjoy the space. We held movie nights, yoga, and cooking classes.

I left the job because I was ready to retire. Directing an early education school was not going to be my new career. It made sense to move on from here and let someone else provide educational leadership of this magnificent program. Then, Boston College gave me a call. Although I worked as full-time faculty from 2016-2018, I straddled both worlds, work and leisure. One of the things I noticed over the years was there's never enough time to get things done. Many people I talk to share this feeling. We ask, "Where did the time go?" or "Where did the day go?" I concluded that time moves at the same steady pace, but people move slower. Therefore, the day goes faster. Days feel shorter, weeks flew along, and it was hard to believe the things I did were much farther away than I could remember. But it's okay now that I'm fully retired.

The Boston College (BC) experience was the best. I tell people all the time, if I knew it would be this good, I would have sought a faculty position sooner. Before BC, I had taught at three other colleges (BU, Bay Path, and UMass Boston) as adjunct faculty. My strategy was to gain classroom experience to teach while in retirement. When BC came calling, I had been teaching for ten years, albeit part-time, and felt well prepared for the classroom. I loved the flexibility of my schedule and the opportunity it provided for me to give back to the community. I enjoyed being with students, although some were challenging, there were always the gems. Knowing you were helping to shape minds and expand their knowledge is so rewarding. Teaching always keeps me in a learning mode, making sure I am prepared to lecture. Between classes, I would develop my presentations or lessons. Just like life, you don't stand in front of these students and try to wing it.

Similarly, you don't enter retirement without planning. There is no right time to make this change. You must want to stop and not feel any pressure to leave. Some of my friends could take early retirement, and others can't imagine they will ever retire. I'm not sure when Pam and I started to take it seriously, but my guess was after age fifty. Most people don't know what they would do in retirement but know they must keep busy doing something. It's always better to enter retirement on your terms, knowing you did all you could and wanted to do in the work world. Whatever is left to do remains in good hands and in good condition for the next person who follows your steps.

We asked the first big question: Can we afford to stop working? Will we have enough funds to last for the rest of our lives, not knowing how long that would be? What kind of lifestyle do we want? Where would we live? There were so many questions and things to learn. And yet, there was a lot we did not know to ask.

One of the best decisions we made was to seek a financial planner. With her help, she calculated that we would be okay financially based on a projected budget. That means we could enjoy retirement if we took specific actions early. Putting all of the pieces in place was the task at hand. Again, it's a blessing to have several resources. Everyone needs to understand Social Security is totally insufficient!

A part of the strategy was the decision to move South. We chose Charlotte after years of research and visiting potential locations. We could sell our home in Canton, Massachusetts, and move into a new home a few months later. Most of our retirement funds are in investment accounts, with the future cost of living increases projected to keep up with inflation. We were able to eliminate loans and any significant debt. Everything we did was the result of careful and thoughtful planning. Of course, our retirement budget had a few splurges built-in, such as going out for fine dining, entertainment, NBA tickets, and overseas travel and cruises. As we go through the next decade or two, we can see if we have made the right decisions.

So, what was guiding me toward retirement? Unlike my talented wife Pam, who worked in television news her entire career, I kept changing jobs. I did not plan it that way, but I was very fortunate to have had an exciting and fulfilling professional career, as it turned out. I worked at eleven different organizations in four occupational areas over forty-six years.

The chart below indicates where I worked and the start year.

Chart of Jobs

Higher Education Admin 18 years	UConn 1972	Conn College 1974	Colgate 1979	UMass Boston - 1981
Nonprofit Consulting 11 years	Ron Ancrum Consulting - 1990	Ancrum & Solomon - 1993	Third Sector New England - 1998	
Philanthopy 11 years	Associated Grant Makers - 2001	Community Foundation of W. MA - 2009		
Social Service 6 years	Nurtury Learning Lab - 2012	BC School Social Work - 2015		

Most of my jobs were in management or executive-level positions. Again, very fortunate. Without question, it's better to be the "boss" than not. In those roles, I was responsible for leading an organization to achieve success and building a team to help reach that goal. Don't ever think you can accomplish that task by yourself. I always believed you manage things and not people. You control the budget, office procedures, the planning process, etc. When it came to personnel, your role was to cheerlead, motivate, empower, and support. I can't say I was great in this role, but I was not terrible. Most of my staff was excellent. I'm so grateful for all the talented people I had around me. Searching for people more competent and more skilled than myself was the key. Hiring the right people was essential to having a solid team. There were a few mistakes along the way and situations where no matter what I did, it was not a positive experience.

Finding a location with warmer weather was a primary goal: moving to the Caribbean, southern California, or the South. Staying in Boston was out of the question, too cold and too expensive. We thought a lot about where we wanted to live. In 2005, we planned to become "snowbirds," living a portion of the time in St. Croix. Those plans changed for several reasons.

We made a list of places and started to visit the cities we had not seen before. We knew we did not want to be in Florida. Pam's parents moved to Ocala, and to see them, we took many trips there and to Orlando during those years. We also did not want to live in Atlanta, a sprawling city that grew too fast and has traffic issues similar to Boston. My family members had previously lived in Richmond, and we had visited Virginia Beach and Williamsburg. Nice, however, too quiet for us. In the end, we settled on moving to either North Carolina or Maryland.

My mother and sister live outside Baltimore, so we gave Annapolis, Maryland, a good look. It was close enough to Washington, DC, for a large city environment. At the time, Pam's sister and brother lived in the eastern part of North Carolina, becoming a target state. I had traveled to Charlotte, Winston Salem, and Greensboro on business and liked what I saw. The other factor that tipped the scale to Charlotte was because we wanted a city with professional sports teams. Eventually, we created a chart listing all the pros and cons of the cities on our list. Charlotte was the winner, and we felt it was the right decision.

Healthcare is a top concern for retired Americans. We made sure the city we chose had quality medical centers. Medical costs are complicated to estimate, but we know expenses are too high in general. Making sure we had health insurance that allowed for out-of-network doctors was critical. We also looked at the higher education institutions in the area as a potential place for me to teach and for cultural programs.

My early vision of retirement was to sit on my porch in a rocking chair with a glass of lemonade or sweet tea whenever I want. I almost got it right. Instead of the front porch, it's the back deck which is a good size, and the backyard has plenty of trees along the boundaries to provide privacy. My chairs are not rocking but comfortable, and my choice of beverage might be coffee in the morning and a glass of wine in the evening.

After the experience we had with other family members, we downsized our house. You don't need to be a hoarder to accumulate many things, and we had plenty of stuff to purge. We decided to move into a smaller, single-level house. No more going up and down stairs. If we decide later to stay in this house until we get older, called *aging in place*, we can do so, but we also wanted the option to move into an assisted living facility.

Planning for the future is difficult because you don't know how your needs might change. We do not have any other family members nearby to help us. That's why we are taking steps to purge items we held onto for sentimental reasons and unload stuff we no longer use. We learned through assisting my Mom that there are four activities to determine if you need help as a senior: 1) personal care, 2) household chores, 3) eating healthy meals, and 4) money management. When any of these are challenging, you should seek help. Retirement should be a time for you to relax and use your time to do whatever you want at this stage of life.

As I mentioned, we were more concerned about the financial question of whether we would have enough resources throughout our lives. Today, nearly 25% of all seniors will live to age ninety, according to the Social Security Administration. Many of us worry that we will outlive our money. You create a budget, which others suggest, based on an unsubstantiated calculated guess. Understanding and realizing your monthly income after you leave employment is a huge guess. But without planning and going through this exercise, you can't make the best decisions for you and your family.

The decision to accept a faculty position at BC was absolutely the right choice. I could have decided not to teach, but you need to adjust when you believe your pathway is predetermined. We had planned on Pam working after relocating to Charlotte, but it was no longer necessary and she was pleased. The pressure of finding something she would enjoy after her career in the media was daunting. If we wanted to engage in a consulting project, we created Ancrum Strategic Advisors.

The Fourth Quarter brings about changes in your habits. We would go to the movies on Tuesday since it was discounted down to only $5.00 per person. We can stay out late on a weeknight because we are no longer working. In the retirement years, it's essential to keep busy. I find myself watching more TV than I had hoped. When you do that, you are not active and, depending on what you watch, may not stimulate your mind. Of course, some TV is good for just relaxing. In later chapters, I will discuss my list of things to keep busy.

I talk to some of my friends who are still working, and a few feel they will probably never retire. I'm often unsure what's behind their responses, but I can't imagine not ever retiring. By the time I decided to take that step at the end of 2015, I had enjoyed working but was exhausted, just plain tired. What Nurtury did to benefit the children attending the center and families at Bromley-Heath Housing Development was rewarding, but I no longer had that drive and energy.

To not work for possibly twenty more years is absolutely scary. That's a long time to stay busy socially and live an active life. Not having anywhere you must go, no meetings, or no community problems to solve, leaves a void in your day-to-day calendar. But, it's easy to fill the days and nights with the exciting activities you choose. How you keep on moving to be physically and mentally active is critical. I now have more opportunities to volunteer, just have a simple lunch with a friend, or plan an event for one of the member organizations I support. At times, I feel like I have an abundance of time. Other times, it's almost too busy. The difference is I am in total control of what I do. I'm so happy to be in this place. **For me, retiring has been great!**

CHAPTER 4

Health: Part One

The pitchman in a famous television commercial likes to say, "Here's the real deal." Having a chronic illness can change everything. It pushes its way to the top of the agenda in everything you do. It changes plans, dreams, and realities. It is the reason I'm writing these words. Perhaps my motivation to be open will give others a way to develop a strategy and live with this kind of uncertainty. My thoughts may also help you better care for a loved one. Unfortunately, when we get to this stage of life, many begin to experience health issues. If you don't plan on it, you should. The following is an account of what this period has been for me and my health. The subject of my health is very lengthy, so it's divided into three parts.

My primary health problem is Pulmonary Arterial Hypertension (PAH), a chronic and progressive disease of the lungs. There is no cure, no getting better. Over time, it will only get worst and limit my physical activities. The best I can hope for is to sustain an active life and learn to live with this medical problem in the best way possible. Although it can lead to heart failure, I mostly experience severe shortness of breath. I had read that the estimated life expectancy is five years. I had no idea when that countdown began for me or how much longer it will continue. More recent information suggests a person can live much longer than five years.

So how healthy was I before now? It's hard for me to remember things about my childhood years. My mother tells me I had the usual childhood illnesses (chickenpox, measles, etc.), and allergies, which left rashes all over my legs and arms. In college, every fall and spring, I would sneeze like crazy from the tree pollen, leading to bronchial coughing. It didn't help that UConn was in the country, in the middle of lots of woods, trees, and fields.

At age twenty-five, I was diagnosed with Sarcoidosis, an incurable chronic disease. Since then, my breathing has progressively gotten worse, with periodic inflammation of the lungs. In 1981, studies showed that most people live with sarcoidosis for just ten years. The average age of death is thirty-nine. More recently, data shows that less than 10% have cases that could become fatal. I have learned there are cases, like mine, where it has little impact on one's lifespan. At fifty, I was still very active in playing softball and tennis, which kept me in relatively good physical shape. I also spent lots of effort thinking about my nutrition.

In 1974, I stopped smoking, so I was already on the right track. After reading "Cooking with Mother Nature" by Dick Gregory, I stopped eating beef and pork. My daily routine consisted of homemade granola (the best you'll ever have), yogurt for lunch with wheat germ and fruit, and salad for dinner. I lost weight, which was not the objective, but I gained lots of energy and awareness. After two months, I did not eat any fried foods, no meats, nothing with sauces, etc. I have since gone back to eating everything except beef and pork.

Fast forward to the 21st century. In 2006, I had a minor stroke called a TIA (Transient Ischemic Attack). I woke up that morning, and my hand was shaking like crazy. Staying home was not an option because I was on a panel of speakers for a conference plenary session that morning. I would grasp the chair while sitting on the stage and the podium to calm the shaking when speaking. Finally, it was over, and I immediately found a quiet corner so I could think about what to do. I drove home, called the doctor to get an immediate appointment, and called my wife for help. My doctor sent me to the emergency room, where the diagnosis was stroke symptoms. They could not tell why, I can only conclude that stress was a leading factor.

My doctor tested me for prostate cancer after my PSA test score was above average. Fortunately, the discovery was at an early stage. In May of 2008, I elected to have surgery rather than radiation treatment. I talked with other men who had survived this cancer and read as much as possible to understand what options were available. Because we caught it early, I decided to have surgery. Just cut it out and be done with it was my attitude. Unfortunately, it happened during the 2008 NBA Playoffs and Championships. The Boston Celtics played, and I missed seeing the final game in person from my Garden seats. You don't know how I hated to miss that game. I was a big fan of the team and Paul Pierce.

Since then, I noticed my breathing was becoming more

challenging—climbing stairs, walking any long-distance, and exercising was problematic. Working at the Nurtury Learning Lab was a health struggle, especially while constructing the early learning center. The dust particles at the site were overwhelming. It also seemed that I would get very ill every winter with the influx of viruses and dry air from heating systems. The only treatment that worked was to get an antibiotic for the inflammation and Prednisone, a steroid, to clear the air passages.

Since relocating to North Carolina in 2016, I have been in the hospital three times. The first time was December 27-29, 2016. Pam drove me to the hospital following a few days of me feeling tired and unable to breathe sufficiently. We were supposed to fly up to Boston to celebrate New Year's Eve with our crew. How disappointed I was not to be physically fit to travel.

My second trip to the hospital was less than three months later, March 5-7, 2017. The situation was similar to the previous time. I was at our new home in Charlotte during college spring break. Within days, I was struggling to breathe and not feeling well again. We arrived at the hospital that evening. By midnight, due to the infectious nature of my sickness, I was moved to the ICU. Within days of getting out of the hospital, I had to travel back to Boston, still not fully recovered and experiencing shortness of breath as I navigated through the airport, getting on and off the plane despite using travel assistance, and finally walking to the apartment from the taxi drop off in front of the building. I had to take my time walking and stopping when necessary.

Following these two trips to the hospital, we wondered if the problem was the air quality in our home. Could the problem be the dry air from the heating system? We took several steps to alleviate this issue by having an air quality test for possible pollutants or allergens. Pam rented a machine to clean all the carpets. We also purchased two air filter machines, placed humidifiers in several rooms, and changed the filters on the house HVAC system after it was inspected and cleaned. None of that worked entirely.

I finally had a Cardiac Catherization Test on December 5, 2017, which verified I had PAH. Treating PAH had become the priority, which meant trial by error to find the best medicine and dosage for my condition. Besides the effects of the meds, I also had to think about staying clear of other people who might be contagious with a virus and, therefore, must carefully plan where and how I travel. My regular travel routine was the back and forth between Boston and Charlotte. To avoid being in the wrong environment, I decided not to renew my faculty contract at Boston College and enter full retirement in May 2018. Earlier diagnosis by my doctors prepared me for needing oxygen or possibly having a lung transplant. Now, I must adjust to a new normal. It's up to me to take care of myself. With the help of my family, my general thoughts were, I'll do just fine.

Most afternoons and evenings, I'm at home sitting in a chair, watching TV, eating dinner, reading, and working in the home office without help. To live with this health issue, I must exercise, change my diet, keep mentally active, and be less stressed. I started Qi Gong, a form of meditation and slow-flowing movements, very light stuff, hoping it might help my breathing. That lasted a few weeks. We just purchased some light weights to work on arm strength. But, as I said before, I'm not particularly eager to exercise. Changing food and diet is much easier for me, and that works.

Then, on October 24-26, 2018, I took a trip to visit my friend, Alan, in Oklahoma City. I had a great time eating out and going to a Thunder versus Celtics basketball game. That night, we went out for dinner at Mickey Mantle's, a favorite spot of his, then to the game in a limo. It was a great match, two good teams, both playoff contenders at the beginning of the season. Throughout most of the game, the Thunder led and looked like they would win. But never underestimate your opponent and what can happen in the fourth quarter of a game. With a few minutes remaining, and the Thunder still up, Alan started to celebrate (much too soon as it turned out). You know how it is with us brothers. We start boasting and bragging. That all changed in the final two minutes and the Celtics went on to win 101 to 95. I got bragging rights that night. After the game, we went back to Mickey's for a cocktail and met some of Alan's friends.

The next day, I boarded a flight to return home, and on Monday, I started to experience severe breathing issues. As I looked back on the trip, the flights to and from Charlotte went through Atlanta airport, so they were long trips. The hotel room was excellent but stuffy due to the heating system and the smoke in the air. Cigarette and cigar smoke at the restaurant probably did me in. Yes, they still allow smoking in bars in Oklahoma.

Days later, we were sitting at home on Halloween night watching TV. Most of the day, I had not been feeling well. Most days, I manage to get by, provided I don't overexert myself. But that night, I was struggling a lot. I went to lay down to rest, hoping to take it easy, allowing it time to go away. It got so bad I had to sit down after walking ten steps. We got in the car and again drove to the hospital. As Pam sped down the street, I asked her to slow down because I found it hard to breathe, as if the speed was making it more difficult. I did not want to go to the hospital as I had done in 2017 and 2018. I never want to go to the hospital.

I also did not think I could last without some medical treatment. It was the right decision. I spent two nights in the hospital and returned home, this time with an oxygen concentrator. Yes, I was tethered to a machine with tubing to get enough oxygen in my body. I knew this day was coming, but not this soon. My life is forever changed, which led me to start a journal.

From My Journal:

November 2018 - *These past few months had been the most challenging and life-altering in my life. Shortly after I came home from the hospital, we had a visit from our niece, Dede, and her husband, Charles. We all, including Pam's sister Phyllis, went out for dinner, and I had to bring the large oxygen concentrator into the car. This machine is called portable, and to some extent, it is, but it is still 50 pounds to lug. We left the machine in the car, and I walked to the restaurant, knowing I might need to stop to catch my breath. I must admit, I was not ready for the world to see me with an oxygen machine.*

I was looking forward to receiving a smaller, portable oxygen concentrator. This would make travel out of the house easier, especially longer trips via car, air, or cruise. After I got it, I took a test run by going to a luncheon event and a jazz concert. I did not expect that I would need to use the machine the whole time sitting but would use it in the car, as needed. The Inogen machine was extremely helpful. A larger, heavier, and more cumbersome oxygen concentrator machine delivered from the hospital is the primary equipment I used at home and for the more extensive car trips. Whereas I use the smaller, more portable device when I go shopping, attend meetings, and attend church on Sunday.

Sleeping at night is good. As usual, I wake up several times to use the bathroom. Going back to sleep is generally not a problem. I started using the home oxygen concentrator all night. I easily get tired during the day. If I sit still too long, I just fall asleep. Watching TV at night is a joke. Most of the time, I drift off whether I'm on the couch, in a chair, or in bed. I believe I could fall asleep standing up. It doesn't matter.

When I'm sitting still, I can shut off the oxygen machine and just take it easy. When moving around, it's much better to have supplemental air. The amount of oxygen is measured in liters per minute. I need at least level 3 these days. My breathing is okay as long as the oxygen saturation levels don't drop too low (below 85%). Fortunately, within minutes, I recover, and the levels go back up.

November 28, 2018 - I went out for an appointment to look at a possible venue for an upcoming meeting and felt out of breath when I returned to the car. Usually, after using Prednisone, I would feel much better and can walk without any assistance. This time, that wasn't the case. Not sure if I should worry about it or not.

Is the use of a concentrator making me more dependent on getting oxygen? I can walk around the house without it, but when going out in public, I seem to need it. Is this just a matter of increased anxiety or heightened awareness that I'm wearing these tubes to my nose? Or, are my lungs so bad that I need the machine more often than not?

I also had experienced handshaking similar to when I had the TIA. It happens periodically, and I notice it more when drinking a beverage, particularly using my right hand. I always understood that the human body is a system, and when one part begins to fail, it affects another part. So, what's next?

During the first few months, I had not told many people about my medical condition, and I tried to hide it a little when we are out socially. I'm sure that would change with time. I would bring the concentrator to the restaurant but take the nasal cannula off after I sat down. I used to not bring the portable machine with me into the church.

By this fall, I had a new primary care physician, Dr. Ellis, in Charlotte. I also found a new Pulmonologist in Lexington at Wake Forest Hospital, almost a one-hour drive northeast of Charlotte. Between the two doctors, they were helping me find the best treatment and monitoring my situation. In addition, I kept my notes and kept an eye on my mental well-being.

From My Journal:

December 18, 2018 — I had my appointment with a new doctor to address the PAH. This was important for two reasons. First, now that I'm permanently in NC, going back to Boston to see my cardiologist was no longer viable. Second, I was just hospitalized on Halloween and now home with oxygen. It's very obvious, the problem with my lungs has gotten worst.

The bottom line after this visit, I need to make some decisions regarding further treatment. Pam and I are looking at the option presented by a Pulmonology doctor here in NC to seek lung transplant surgery. This will be a tough decision and needs to be made soon. The age limit for lung transplantation is 70. (I was 69.)

How will I process this information and not get depressed? Putting my trust in God will be a start. I have always said, when that time comes, I'll be ready. As I said before, life has been good, and I've been blessed. I must understand that you live the life you are handed because you can't do much more. Not everyone lives until they are 90 years old. To reach 70 or more is more significant than I thought when I was younger because of my health.

Moving forward from this point depends on pushing myself a little, but not too far. I need to understand my boundaries and be willing to gather enough strength to stay active and maintain the right mindset to remain engaged. Going to church on Sundays is essential. Whenever I shook hands with the Pastor after service, he would tell me, "Thanks for making an effort." He could see that I was carrying an oxygen concentrator and could easily justify staying home. I had to learn not to be embarrassed by lugging an oxygen machine or make others around me feel like I was helpless. The more I can keep doing what I do, the better it feels.

CHAPTER 5

Sidelines: Part One

MOST OF MY DECISIONS HAVE BEEN MADE THROUGH SOME CAREFUL PLANNING AND WITH LOTS OF THINKING BEHIND IT. FORTUNATELY, I NEVER FELT I WAS UNDER PRESSURE TO DECIDE; NEVER REACTIONARY OR LOSING FOCUS TO WHAT I WANTED TO ACCOMPLISH OR GAIN.

Sidelines reflect the part of the game that's not really *in* the game. These are the boundaries that surround the playing field or court. Sometimes there are conversations between coaches or players off to the side while the match is going on. The coach also uses the time to process what's on their mind. How to make it better or retain the edge? This is when the decisions can impact the game, and together, Pam and I made plenty of life-changing decisions.

We were planning to leave Boston for more than ten years before it happened. Both of us had enough long cold winter months and preferred moving to a warmer climate. Understand me when I say we wanted to leave. Boston is a great city. It has everything you will need, especially professional opportunities, plenty of arts and culture, sports teams that win championships, shopping, and dining galore. It attracts visitors and college students year-round. We had lots of friends or great colleagues, stayed active with organizations and clubs, and lived in two beautiful homes, first in Dorchester then in Canton. The biggest issue for us was the weather and the high cost of living there. Leaving many great friends behind is a concern, and we need to make new connections.

I especially loved our home in Canton. It had plenty of space, was practical, and not overwhelming. The location was a reasonable distance, both in miles and time, to the drive to downtown Boston. The highway to wherever we needed to go was nearby. Across the street was a state preservation area, woods, and trails. Our neighbors, although very friendly, were a distance apart. The backyard and space in the house were great for throwing parties or hosting a cookout, which we did a fair amount. But it was time to move on.

In the summer of 2016, I was off from teaching at BC, and we were able to find a new house in Charlotte, and move by July. Before that, we settled into a two-bedroom apartment in the University City area for six months. The apartment was a cozy place on the second floor of the building. We never got to know our neighbors or anyone who lived in the complex.

The residential community of our new home was a change for us. We thought we would never live in a suburban residential community. We had lived in the city and suburbs of Boston. Our new residential development, is a community with homes, mostly two-level houses, lining the street with mailboxes aligned and the yards all neatly manicured. It resembled one of those cookie-cutter streets you see on television. From the outside, they all look alike, very uniform.

The house we chose had everything on our checklist: three bedrooms and bathrooms to welcome guests and a private backyard for entertaining. The clincher was a water feature with a soothing look and peaceful sound. The previous owner landscaped the yard as a natural habitat for wildlife, and there is plenty of activity. The birds, butterflies, squirrels, occasional deer, snakes, turtles, and rabbits all keep the yard active. During the summer months, the mating season, the toads are extremely noisy at night. The house was perfect for us in so many ways. It was a single-level home which meant no more stairs to climb. We were able to downsize, at the best cost, with enough space. It was not brand new but not old either.

During a lifetime, you make decisions that determine your journey. Most day-to-day choices will have little impact, such as the one I ask myself often, *what will I have for lunch today?* But then there are the major decisions that can alter what you do, where you go, and how you live.

You might remember *The Adjustment Bureau* with Matt Damon, Emily Blunt, and Anthony Mackie. In the movie, David, the main character, must decide whether to accept his predetermined path to be elected president. His life was not supposed to include Elise, who he meets and falls for instantly. If he defies fate to be with her, it will alter both their careers. I believe we all have a predetermined path, but we can choose which road to travel. I can look back on my life and wonder, what if I made a different decision about my college major? When I was in high school, I thought about being an architect. I took drafting and art classes, science, and math. However, in my senior year, that interest changed to music. While in graduate school, what if I had accepted an arts management internship in Hartford? In what direction would my career have gone? What if Pam and I never moved to Boston to work, stayed in Connecticut longer, and followed her television news reporting and anchoring career in another city, not in the northeast? Life for us, the friends, and professional contacts would be very different.

In 2010, I did something I always wanted to do. I guess this is considered *free will*. There was no justification for doing it, but I did it anyway. It was not something I needed other than to satisfy my interest. I was beyond the point of having a midlife crisis, or what most of us think is a point of living out an adult fantasy. For me, it was to own (again) a sports car. Previously, I had a bright yellow Karmann Ghia when I started working at Connecticut College. This time I bought a brand-new Audi TT. I kept my Nissan Murano, so I owned two cars. I drove the Audi when the weather was good. Otherwise, it was in the garage, away from the cold and snow. The SUV was for stormy weather or to lug boxes and other items in a large enough cargo area. For practical reasons, I still have an SUV today. I sold the Audi in 2015 before we moved. Staying with an SUV was the right decision. But not until I got owning a sports car out of my system. At least, I thought it had passed. Somedays, I wish I still had a sports car.

Most decisions result from careful planning and lots of thinking behind them. Fortunately, I never felt I was under pressure to make a quick decision, never reactionary or losing focus on what I wanted to accomplish or gain. One of the decisions I made with the highest risk was when I decided to leave my position at UMass Boston and start my consulting firm. I resigned from a job with a good salary, benefits, and success, to being less certain if I would find clients, earn enough money, all without employment benefits. I described that decision as "going out on a limb." It was a considerable risk that Pam was also willing to take with me. I gave myself six months to put things in order. I talked with friends who already had a successful consulting business, which led to my startup affiliation with a highly successful consulting firm that helped me get going.

Fortunately, Pam was doing well at work and making an excellent salary, so we got rid of debt and lowered expenses. I gave UMass Boston a three-month departure notice that allowed me time to announce my career change publicly. Going public led to my first two contracts before I entirely departed my employment. My situation was not the norm, but I felt I made the right decision because I planned. In the end, that decision somehow led to all the places I worked and the positions I held that followed.

When you plan, you are more focused. Focus is easier when you approach it from positive thinking rather than negative. If you begin the process from a negative position, you become unfocused or more consumed with that problem and not on your interest. The goal is to advance professionally. Focus on how a new challenge looks and what you must do to get that opportunity.

There are many books and articles on how to make good decisions. Some provide step-by-step guidance. When it came to career decisions, it was essential to believe my work was making a difference in people's lives and that I was where I was supposed to be, on my predetermined path. I generally plan every aspect of my life, not leaving things to chance or making non-rational or spontaneous decisions. I got into the habit of being creative while applying logical processes. Not every opportunity is the right one, so you need to assess if your choice will place you where you're supposed to be next. Here is my list of the nine **most** important things you'll need to decide in your lifetime:

1. Education – College/Major/Training
2. Career – Jobs
3. Social Life – Lifestyle/Friendships
4. Love – Dating/Marriage
5. God – Religion/ Spiritual/Faith
6. Financial – Managing Funds
7. Home – Where to Live
8. Retirement – When to Quit Working
9. Health – Care/Nutrition/Exercise

Not all information you receive is good news or factually accurate. People share information they may have received in confidence, then turn around to spread rumors, repeat untruths, or express their own beliefs with no factual basis whatsoever. You will hear or read about the negative things going on around you all the time. You'll listen to it in a news report or as gossip from your contacts. Occasionally, you hear about some positive stuff, but not enough. I try hard not to pass on bad news and only uplift the positive information. I try to nurture meaningful relationships and not support anything that creates a division. The divide in America, especially politically, needs significant repair. So, what's happening in Charlotte? Maybe we should have checked on the crime, politics, or racism in this city before purchasing a home.

From My Journal:

Don't Bring Me No More Bad News (Fall 2018) - *Today was a good day simply because I was able to attend church. It's been 11 days since going into the hospital, nine days since returning home. During this time, the mid-term elections were held, another mass shooting occurred, and massive fires are burning forests, homes and killing people. There's so much bad news.*

We have been saying this for two years, and our 45th president has lost his mind if he had one to lose. He berated the news media, engaged in name calling of Republicans attributing their loss to not supporting him, and threatened to shut down the government if the Democrats investigate him—too much stuff to address each issue. After the 2018 election, my biggest concern was that we are heading for an even more contentious period now that the Dems control the US House. It's simply going to get uglier. In the meantime, people are suffering. So many without homes and help after the hurricanes and now fires.

The other day, I realized that crime is an everyday occurrence in Mecklenburg County. Watching the news, you hear news reports on random shootings, robberies, guns entering schools, and people being murdered. It made me wonder is crime growing in Charlotte as the population grows? There have been over 6,000 violent crimes committed this year, over 100 homicides.

This city seems to be at a loss for addressing this issue. Nothing is getting done to improve schools because there's no agreement on a strategy, and most of the usual actions cost more money than the system can afford. I would ask why youth feel the need to bring a weapon to school, knowing full well it's against policy and could get you suspended if not shot. Talking to the youth is essential to finding a reasonable solution. Other cities know that law enforcement presence, good undercover work, and community oversight can help to reduce crime. Many of the suspects are known criminals with records.

Keeping the youth on the right track requires good after-school and summer programs. Besides, having a solid mentor can make a world of difference. I have had several mentors who helped guide me along my path throughout my life. I believe mentoring is an organic process, meaning it develops naturally. Both people decide, without necessarily saying anything, to continue to build a mutually beneficial relationship. The mentor helps the mentee, and the mentee provides gratification to the mentor. Mentorship programs can start that process, but it's challenging to create the kind of match that will last forever.

One of my earliest mentors was a Republican, Brahmin, lawyer, and politician. I can remember him hiring me to work, raking leaves, and fixing up an old house he purchased. He often talked with me and my friend, Bruce, about going to college. He helped me get into the University of Connecticut, where Bill Trueheart worked in the admissions office. Bill became one of my mentors. He grew up just down the street from where I grew up. He became president at Bryant College and when I had my consulting business, one of my first clients was Bryant College. I was part of a team with my first boss, Jan Hersey, in college admissions and the former UConn director of admissions, John Vlandis (Bill's old boss), who referred me to that first admissions job at Connecticut College. These relationships, linked in different ways, were vital to me in the early years.

From 1993 until today, my mentor has been Hubie Jones, Dean Emeritus of the BU School of Social Work and respected community leader. Hubie hired me as a consultant when he was interim president at Roxbury Community College (RCC). He returned to his tenured position at Boston University and recommended that I take over as the Interim President at RCC until the next hired president could start. Over the years, I have reached out to Hubie to discuss my career plans. More importantly, he is a friend. In my efforts to give back, I became a mentor to his son. Hubie was my prime reference for my teaching job at Boston College. The Dean at BC was so highly impressed by his supporting letter. Hubie also recommended I provide some consulting services to Higher Ground, an organization he founded, which I did during my last academic year at Boston College. Our relationship is special and continues today.

I know some other men and women helped me along the way, but these three were probably the most integral. So, who have I helped? There have been young men and women who have introduced me to others as their mentor. Some I still keep in touch with even today. Helping others is what God asks of us. It does not always come in the form of treasure, but using my talents, providing guidance, or opening a door for them to advance is something I fully believe. Some of the young men and women I have mentored go back to my early years at Connecticut College.

These relationships develop over time. You may not know immediately, and until you can reflect on it, realize the importance. The most gratifying part is to watch a mentee grow. Some of them complete a doctorate, take on a high-powered job, and succeed in ways you could not have imagined. My mentees' accomplishments make me smile.

Life is an unexpected journey that starts as a dream but later is a reality. You can only know what your life was when you can look back to see what you have done. All of your decisions culminate into a fork in the road where you decide which of these options is your choice, and you hope you made the best choice. Often, it's not a matter of right or wrong, just different.

I had no idea I would have the type of jobs I had and the varied professional opportunities. Things I might want do not always happen, but I have no regrets. At one point, I thought I might be a musician, but honestly, I did not work hard enough to do that full-time. I look back, and I like what I see. I can be proud of what I did and see my mistakes along the way, and there were plenty of them. Despite my health issues, I can still travel, go out for dinner, listen to music, engage in volunteer work, and enjoy conversations and friendships with other couples, especially with other Black men.

Spending time talking with another brother is special. One of those I sought out to spend time with was Willie Jones. We both attended the same church back in Boston. I was a mentor to his youngest son when his son was in high school. I got to know Willie through his wife, Pam. She and I served on a Diversity Committee coordinated through The Hyams Foundation. My wife got to know Willie when they worked on building relationships with a fellow church in Wellesley, Massachusetts. Ironically, we both moved from Boston to Charlotte. Willie uses his expertise to work with the community and churches in the area, to address housing and community development. I thought I might do the same with educational programs for youth.

Since Willie has been living in Charlotte, he completed a Master of Theological Studies degree and is now an ordained minister. I explained to Willie that I "designated" him as a brother to talk with from time to time. There is no real agenda but having someone to open up to when you need it is vital. I hope this works for both of us.

Developing strong ties with other Black men is rewarding, almost necessary as a Black man. These ties can be hard to come by because you can often feel as though you're competing, especially when you are young and trying to impress the ladies.

That's great about the Fourth Quarter. You're no longer trying to impress others or be in charge. Instead, it's about fitting in and cherishing the fellowship. Even if you did not grow up in the same city or community, you can reminisce about the old days and have something in common.

Chapter 6

Music: The Road to Quintessence and Beyond

Ever since I can remember, I have always loved music. Although I do not play or perform anymore, I listen to music, mostly jazz, all the time. Music gave me purpose. Much of my early achievements in life came from music. It kept me protected from the harmful elements of hanging out with the wrong crowd. All I could think about and wanted to do was play my instrument.

I started playing trumpet in the seventh grade and performed in various groups like Up with People, Silver Falcon Drum & Bugle Corps, and the Stamford Young People's Symphony Orchestra. In the summer, there were theater pit orchestras. During the school year, I played in almost all the music organizations. My interest in jazz developed during my junior high school years, listening to Art Blakeley and the Jazz Messengers, Lee Morgan, Coltrane, and Miles Davis. Bruce and I would go all over the city to perform. We both had old used cars, he had his first, which took us wherever we needed to go. We always got a laugh when his passenger door would fly open going around a curve, usually to the surprise of other passengers.

Stamford is a suburb of New York City, so it was easy to take the train into Grand Central Station and the subway downtown to Washington Square and the Village Gate nightclub. There was always plenty of jazz around and local musicians. We were also not too far from the Newport Jazz Festival in the summer.

I graduated with a Bachelor of Music degree from the University of Connecticut to study music theory and composition under Charles Whittenberg and Hale Smith. I started playing piano in jazz groups during my junior year. As a student, there were many opportunities to orchestrate, arrange and compose music for theater, orchestra, jazz band, and gospel choir.

Of all the music projects I worked on, the largest production was the multi-media staging of The Who's

"Tommy," performed by the School of Fine Arts at UConn. I was the Music Arranger and electric piano and French horn player in the eleven-piece band (a part rock group with horns). The show had dancers, actors, singers, and slide projections in the background. Performances were staged on campus and at the Bushnell Auditorium in Hartford to rave reviews. If they had received the license, the show would have gone on tour.

After graduation, I decided to travel to San Francisco with my girlfriend and her dog in a Volkswagon. I thought the west coast style of music was more suited to my interest, and my ambition was to write music scores for movies. My idol was Quincy Jones. He composed and arranged for everyone and was an award-winning movie score writer for years. After short stops in San Francisco and Seattle, we returned home. However, it ended up not as expected, an exciting three-week cross-country journey. If you have never driven across the country, you're missing an experience like no other.

I could have returned home to Stamford, where I had family and people I knew, especially other musicians. But that was not what I wanted. I also could have moved to New Jersey and lived with my mom. It would have provided support while I figured out what to do next. But that, too, was not what I wanted. I instead returned to UConn and found a job in the area. Without a "real job" and career plans, I decided to apply for enrollment in the MA degree in Music Theory and Composition.

From 1972-74, I had a band called Ankh, which was received well by audiences on college campuses. During that same period, I joined the Black Voices of Freedom Gospel Choir (BVF) on campus. Gospel music was always of interest, based on memories of singing in a church choir as a kid. But as an adult, it was something that became a valuable part of my work. BVF was an excellent choir and one that continues today. I sang in the baritone/bass section, and it provided an opportunity for me to write a few selections, which later got recorded by the choir for its first album.

I never completed the master's degree program in music at UConn. Instead, I left Storrs (CT) and moved down the road to New London to work at Connecticut College. The gospel music experience I received at UConn enabled me to help create and support choirs at Connecticut College and five years later at Colgate University. I guess this was when I realized music would not be my full-time profession. Still, I continued performing whenever and wherever I could.

My greatest accomplishment in music was the recording of *Quintessence*, with a band of the same name. The album was recorded in 1980 and released in 1981. The music genre was jazz, Latin, and funk, and all the music was composed and arranged by me. Unfortunately, the band broke up in 1987, we had just got back together after a period of not performing. Pam and I moved to Boston from Hartford. I would make the two-hour drive on weekends for rehearsals and plan our next push to become well-known. I soon learned that members of the band did not share my interest. Everyone wanted to continue playing, but they did not want to travel. About this time, band members had children and spending a weekend in

Boston was not in the picture. Ultimately, the thought of being away from home was not ideal.

I was distraught, and we never played as a band again. There were plenty of musicians I could have recruited in Boston, obviously with the Berklee College of Music nearby. I sang in the choir at church for several years. I also wrote a song for a unique Easter program Pam and I organized. But my schedule got busy with other responsibilities. Similar to my former band members, I now had a child to care for and I entered graduate school again, this time for an MS degree in Public Affairs.

Today, the album is a record collector's item on Discogs. Collectors want it because it's so rare. Discogs is the only marketplace where the album is sold, to my knowledge. I also want to believe people who have heard it seriously enjoy it as well. In 2008, a guy called me to see if I had copies of the album. I agreed to sell him 200 copies, and then months later, found it available to buy on his website, Rarebro Records. In 2012, I spotted a blog, Private Press, discussing the album. Some of the comments are: "Nice, pleasant groove. Good summer afternoon music." I posted to the blog to ask how he heard about the album. Katonah wrote, "Wow, really pleased you dropped by Ron. Seriously, this one, a killer album all the way." Katonah is in London. He picked up a copy in New York, still sealed. "It's quite a special album with collectors." Reading this was very gratifying.

Where does that leave me today? I said I would start to write music again when I retired. Now I'm not sure if I will.

The industry has changed so much, and my piano skills (they were never great) are questionable. My hearing and singing skills are less than they were, and I rely on them to create a phrase or harmony. I feel I have one more song inside of me to share. The problem is, who will play it? I need to take all the music I have written to date and get them in a publishable format.

Now, I just listen to music. We go out to hear jazz all the time. I still have a massive collection, both vinyl records, and CDs. Since retiring, I have formed Charlotte Jazz Buzz (CJB). We function as a book club, listen to a selected artist in advance, and come together to discuss the music and related topics (culture, history, influences, etc.) This club is in its third year. We have listened to and discuss such artists as Terence Blanchard, Les McCann, Wayne Shorter, Miles Davis, Norman Brown, Ben Williams, and more.

One of the most exciting meetings was held jointly with Pam's book club. We listened to the *Round Midnight* soundtrack by Herbie Hancock, read *Sophisticated Giant (the life and legacy of Dexter Gordon)* by Maxine Gordon, and watched the movie *Round Midnight*, starring Dexter. All with discussion and food, of course.

On November 9, we produced a concert called *Gospel & Jazz: Coming Together*. The afternoon was our regular meeting, but this time was held at Little Rock AME Church Cultural Center. Willie Jones facilitated the conversation. In his formidable style, he gave a history lesson on the openness of churches to secular music in the church.

That night, we had a concert with out-of-town guest musicians. Greg Groover, Jr., who recently released his recording, *The Negro Spiritual Songbook, Volume One,* and Kersten Stevens, whose most recent recording was, *Inspire Me,* brought their respective talents to bear. Accompaniment was by a local trio led by Lovell Bradford, also serving as the music director. I wrote on my Facebook page, "*Last Night was the most exciting and spirited concert I have ever been a part of.*" We packed the room with over 120 folks who, judging by the applause and comments, thoroughly enjoyed the performance.

I can't express how much that performance meant to me. Everything we planned fell right into place. You start with an idea or a dream, try to put it together one piece at a time, check and double-check that what you're doing will work as you plan, and then bang! It's here. The audience loved the music, gave standing ovations, and had nothing but praise after. It was a success. *Now what? Should I do this again?*

Playing music provided a balance in my life from the busy and often stressful life at work. In music, I could be creative and have fun. I love the feeling you get when the group is sounding good, everyone is at their best, and it just grooves or cooks. Jazz music combines part orchestration with mostly spontaneity and improvisation. The musicians are like a club, speaking the same language but with a secret handshake. You know what to listen for and are ready for things you had not heard before.

If you have ever been a musician or artist of any form, you can understand why they continue until they can no longer perform. It keeps them alive. Now, I can only dream what my life might have been like to be a full-time musician. It requires lots of commitment—daily hours of practice, late-night and hectic lifestyle, multiple days on the road traveling, and unless you're well-known, less pay and no retirement fund. What if I had made music my career? What would I be doing, and where would I be living? Probably, somewhere outside of Los Angeles.

As I see it, I probably would have finished my graduate degree in music to teach at a university while writing music and playing gigs here and there. Or maybe if I had stayed in San Francisco, I would've found a way to play my trumpet, not piano. My journey would have been very different.

What I miss most is writing music. I should have continued to compose, but it was hard not to have a reason or musicians looking for a song to perform. I would always tell myself that I'll get back to writing. Now that I am retired, I don't have an excuse for not trying. Creating a piece of music is so gratifying. I have heard Herbie Hancock tell others you have the same twelve notes to work with and strung together, they form a melody. The musician harmonically bridges them to blend tones and layers with varying rhythms to complete the story he wishes to convey. When you get to hear it all together in whatever arrangement, it should make you feel good inside. I listen to the *Quintessence* album and feel that same joy as when it was first released.

Chapter 7

Health: Part Two

Aging is a process that is hard to plan for, even though you know it's coming. Is aging just about the years that pass by or about your physical being and mindset? By the time you reach the Fourth Quarter, you will notice a change in who you are. It can happen at any point and will be different for each person. Physically, you begin to look older. Your face begins to wear the miles you traveled, and the wrinkles, sagging, bags under the eyes, and weight gain, etc. There was a point when people would say to me, " . . . and you look great for your age." That does not happen anymore, and nor should I expect it. Mentally, your memory is not as sharp. Your body says you're not young anymore, and yet your mind thinks you're the same. Don't even think about trying to do the things you used to do.

January 1, 2019, was my first New Year's Day since retiring. Time had flown by quickly, and not all news is good news. At the top of the list to address were my health issues. That week we went out for dinner on Saturday with friends. I found the walk into and out of the restaurant to be a strain. My dependency on oxygen seemed to have increased. I can sit for a while without it and move a little, but most of the time, I need extra air. My hand shakes a little, my feet feel a bit swollen, and my body feels weak. I check my oxygen saturation and blood pressure periodically to make sure I'm doing okay. But there were signs that my health problems were getting more serious.

From My Journal:

I have not thought about any resolutions for 2019. Whatever I should or want to do has already been decided. My health is my top priority. I'm trying to fulfill all our travel plans for this year and complete some of the retirement plans on my extensive list of things. I don't need to add anything to the list since I fully expected the list would take at least five years to complete. I'm not sure if I have that much time.

Pam gave me a book to read, entitled "Overcoming Tough Times," which should help me with my resolve with God. I have always said I'm ready when the time comes. I believe I have lived a good and fulfilling life. But I still did not think it will end anytime soon. I can only ask God to strengthen me.

My Pulmonary doctor suggested applying for double lung transplant surgery to determine if I would be a possible candidate, so we went through the process with Duke Medical Center and had an evaluation on January 17, 2019.

The lung transplant evaluation was all day. By the end of the day, the doctor reported that I would not be approved. Most things were favorable, but the risk was more than they would take. Pam and I were not disappointed and generally glad we went through the process. It was a relief to have a decision right away. This would have been a major decision to go forward if approved, requiring tremendous commitment, rehabilitation, and support from family and friends.

So, the plan is to live life as fully as possible and do all I can to create a quality-of-life plan. At the top of the list is to enter some Pulmonary Rehabilitation Center to get me exercising regularly. WALKING IS GOOD! Second, take steps to stabilize the other health problems by eating well and staying positive. My new research and planning began today.

My blood sugar count is high, and we are also monitoring my kidney function, which is also beginning to reach a danger zone. None of this is good. I have been working on my diet and need to do more. Cut out sugar, lower my intake of carbs, cut out coffee (to avoid the use of sugar). Use fruit on cereal instead of sugar and only drink a small glass of juice. Drink more water during the day. Find healthy snacks. More salads and soups for lunch instead of sandwiches. Smaller portions for dessert.

Walking is essential; use the bike, build arm and chest muscles, and do leg exercises to prevent falling.

Most days, I move along with my oxygen and get where I need to go. I take it easy but keep up with essential activities (meetings, social gatherings, chores, etc.). I'm hoping I can stop taking Prednisone. I worry about what it's doing to me. There are just too many side effects from this steroid. Most days, I feel okay. Blood pressure is excellent but can sometimes be high. Oxygen saturation is mostly normal after sitting a few minutes, but at moments of rest can start low.

When I'm struggling, I contact my doctor to get an antibiotic for six days and extra doses of Prednisone. This treatment has worked to improve my breathing. I don't know what causes this change—is it pollen, the heating system, or something else? Or was my anxiety building because I'm getting ready to do something? Usually, in a couple of days, I start to feel better and do what's needed.

What has changed this year are the swollen ankles and feet. I talked with my doctor about it, and he believes it's because of Prednisone. I now try not to wear tight footwear and wear compression socks—just another sign of getting older.

From My Journal:

On June 12, 2019, it became official. I'm a diabetic. It's been passed down through the family, and it finally caught up to me. I thought I ate healthy enough to avoid it, but that did not happen. The doctor, however, believes mine is medicine induced, caused by the meds I took to treat Sarcoidosis and lately, the PAH. It's not bad enough that I have severe breathing issues requiring oxygen. I also have problems with my kidneys, swollen feet and ankles, and tearing eyes. I'm a mess, and yet, I keep going. I can't start feeling bad for myself. Instead, I must keep working to live as healthy a life as possible.

Wake up! I'm getting a belly like my Uncle Don. I swore I would never let that happen. This is not good. I am starting to eat less food, keep lunch to a salad or a smoothie, and exercise. Next week I need to get to the fitness room three times. In between, I need to do sit-ups with Pam's help. Besides exercising and diet, there's not much more I can do. Exercise is critical, diet is vital, sleep is critical, and a positive mind is critical. I still do not eat red meat but have reduced my sugar intake. I am trying to cut back on ice cream. Ice cream is, without a doubt, my addiction. I have started to eat less and find healthy snacks. But I love ice cream and things like chips, if only I could eat them in moderation.

I just started to use a sleep app to monitor how well I sleep. So far, it has told me that I'm awake a lot of the night and get around four hours of sleep, primarily light sleep. I'm at least in bed for 8 hours every night. What I notice about sleeping is, I start to think about something and can't stop, keeping me awake. I'm trying to remember it when I get up. I discovered a trick that helps me stop thinking about it. I write it down on my phone in the notes area. Now it is stored, and I can give it a rest.

The compression socks are helping to keep my feet and ankles from being swollen. The blood sugar count is better, but I must be vigilant not to consume too much sweet stuff or carbs. Most days, I feel fine, but I have this general lull during the day, a need to sleep after dinner, and not getting up early. My eyes are getting worse. Forget about reading anything without reading glasses. I need to wear my regular glasses when watching TV, so I'm not straining them. They still water a lot, and the doctor keeps prescribing new drops. The latest version seems to be better, but I also have been using a compress on my eyes some mornings.

I say this not to make myself or anyone feel bad or down,

but it's a reality that you go through no matter what. For some people, it might start later, but time catches up to you. The longer you can be active, the better. You can only try to keep busy, which means keep moving, and you must engage in things that require you to use your mind. The pain I feel today is normal, and unless it's severe, I don't worry. My eyesight is not as sharp, and I need to see an eye doctor to have them checked. When I look in the mirror, I see an older version of myself, which I should expect.

You know you're getting old when . . .

You can't find your eyeglasses but they're around your neck or on your head.

You are less inclined to want to shave every day.

You call your children by the wrong name.

You can't remember what you did just a few hours ago.

You walk into a room, and you don't remember why you did.

You grunt when getting up and sitting down in a chair.

You fall asleep watching TV at 7:00 PM.

You find yourself repeating the same old stories.

You always talk about the weather.

Chapter 8

Timeouts

We all need time to replenish, re-think, reconnect, or simply rest. In a sports game, you take timeouts to talk about how the game is going and what needs to happen once the game continues. You might switch players on the field or court. The players reach for a sports drink to replenish their electrolytes. They leave the field or court at halftime and return to the locker room to get a needed break.

In life, we use a timeout (or vacation) to get away from a hectic schedule but sometimes return home more exhausted than when we left. In retirement, these trips allow you to change your day-to-day routine. For Pam and me, travel was at the top of the wish list during retirement. The plan was simple; to take at least one major trip per year. Before 2020, we made this a reality with so many trips.

Why wait until retirement to do most of our traveling around the world? No reason except there is more time and flexibility. We always took trips to Bermuda, the Caribbean, Canada, and Mexico. We cruised twice in Europe, docking in Greece, Italy, France, and Spain. My only trip to the continent of Africa was a visit to Kenya (work-related) that got cut short due to a civil war in neighboring Sudan, our target destination. The village where our team of consultants was to conduct a conference was bombed by the Sudanese government the day before we were to arrive. We were sent back home by the United Nations.

Most of the trips in the US were to see friends or family. We also like to take long weekend trips to celebrate birthdays, our anniversary, or other special occasions. We enjoyed the trip to North Carolina's Outer Banks, where we stayed at a lovely B&B and got introduced to Duck Donuts. Our second trip there, we visited Charleston and the studio of highly acclaimed artist, Jonathan Green. Of course, after such a personalized visit, we could not leave without supporting his artwork.

Our first trip after moving to Charlotte was to Sonoma Valley in 2016. We always liked wine and had attended classes on tasting, but this was the beginning of our serious indulgence in wines. We became members at one company and had wine shipped from others. In the city of Sonoma, you can walk from one tasting room to another with ease. One of the stops was at Kamen Wines to enjoy Writer's Block. We made the best decision to hire a driver who took us to three vineyards, Repris Wines being one. The tour at this location was a lesson on making wine but the view from the top of the hillside was even more spectacular. We also had lunch (more like a snack) at DeLoach Vineyards and got hooked on their Pinot Noir Rosé.

While in northern California, we had lunch in Napa Valley with Pam's college buddy, Tanya, and Ingrid, visiting from New Jersey. Also, we stopped outside of San Francisco to have breakfast with my hometown friend, Elliott, and his wife. Keeping up with relationships is cherished by us, especially after many years. All of them attended our wedding back in 1976.

In 2017, Pam and I went on a vacation with our dear friends, the Springers. The destination was one of our favorite places, Bermuda. Not really a Caribbean island, but very much the same feeling. Not only had we vacationed there a lot, but I also managed the island's College Fair for the Ministry of Education for over ten years. We got to visit with our Bermudian friends, the Carey family, who we have known for decades, and received a special gift from them, a bottle of Rum Swizzle. We then searched for the recipe, and when we returned home, we made our own tasty and potent batch.

Traveling with friends is a lot of fun and usually an adventure. We spent one day at Cup Match, an extended cricket match pitting all-star teams from the east end of the island against the west end. After years of watching cricket, I still don't understand the rules. Fortunately, it didn't matter. The festive environment, colorful fashions, food, and gambling (legal only on these two days) was enough to keep anyone entertained.

In April 2018, we flew to the Dominican Republic for a long weekend to celebrate Pam's birthday. Plenty of sun, beach, and dining was on the itinerary. We never left the resort.

In the summer of 2018, we traveled with Phyllis to St. Croix. Although we had a vacation home there, we had not been in years because we had long-term tenants. Since they were finally moving out, we decided to vacation there and start thinking about getting it ready to sell. We did our usual visits to the beach and our favorite spots to eat. One of our evening activities was playing dominoes. Someone had left a large set with as many as fifteen dots on a tile. I had never seen a set this large. As we played, little frogs clung to the exterior of the glass door, likely attracted to the light from inside the condo. We had never seen this before or heard them whistling at night. All-in-all, we loved our condo because it was the perfect place to relax with near perfect weather year-round.

One of the best trips in 2018 was to Florence, Italy, to attend a wedding. Previously, our other trips to Italy were to Rome and several cruise excursions along the Mediterranean Sea. But this event was the most extravagant I have ever experienced. The ceremony took place on a hillside villa estate as a string quartet performed alongside a harp playing today's popular music. The bride was cousin Joe's middle daughter, Eliza. We added a stop in Milan to our itinerary on the front end. However, the trip's highlight was Venice. It was a thrill to see this ancient city with its water canals and quaint cafes. We absolutely love Italian food and wine. Our trip could not have been more timely. Not too long after we visited, the city of Venice was underwater, flooded worse than ever before.

We also took a trip to West Palm Beach, Florida, for Chris and Danielle's wedding. The event was a family affair with a few of their friends. It was nice to see this beautiful young couple tie the knot after years of dating. A year and a half later, they had their first baby, Naomi.

Now that we live in Charlotte, we think differently about travel. Making at least one trip back to Boston per year was added to the must-do list. On Friday, July 26, 2019, we began a twelve-day journey. The trip aimed to visit Erica and a few family and friends along the way. We wanted to avoid flying, so it was an extended road trip. Traveling by car was a way to test my energy level when traveling compared to flying. After we got back, what was apparent was that the long hours in a car could be just as exhausting but more manageable. Going by plane has its advantages and disadvantages. Flying takes less time, generally speaking, but the time sitting in the airport, in the plane cabin, and the limits on what you can bring with you, are all disadvantages.

Along the way, we stopped in Washington, D.C., Connecticut, Rhode Island, and Maryland. In D.C., we stayed at the Gaylord National Resort on the water near Alexandria, Virginia, a beautiful hotel with an enormous atrium. The next day, we went to the Washington Nationals vs. Los Angeles Dodgers baseball game. I grew up as a Brooklyn Dodgers fan as a kid. I knew the players and loved the game. Of course, that meant Jackie Robinson was my baseball idol. Fortunately, I had the opportunity to meet him. Jackie moved his family to North Stamford from New York City after retiring from baseball. His daughter, Sharon, and I are the same age. She attended Stamford High School, the cross-town rival. Whenever she gave a party, the whole town of Black folk knew about it. I remember entering their large house, compared to where I lived, with a sprawling yard and wooded surroundings. Jackie greeted us at the door, probably to make sure we were on the invite list, and welcomed us to his home. Downstairs was a batting cage with lots of baseball memorabilia. Going to a Dodgers game is always special since the team moved out west. As much as I can remember, this was the second time I had the opportunity to watch them play in recent years. The other time was in Boston.

En route to Boston, we decided to stop to visit with cousin Marcia, my grandfather's brother's granddaughter. I think that's right. I have not seen her for almost two years, but we keep in touch via occasional text messages. Three years prior, she took care of my Uncle Donnie and other family members. We talked or saw each other during that year as his health kept getting worse. If it were not for Marcia, Uncle Donnie would have been by himself, with no one checking on him or helping him with daily tasks. As soon as he fell, she called me to say he was in the hospital. For a year, together with Beverly's daughters, Linda and Sharon, we all pitched in to help, but Marcia did the lion's share. Thank God for all of them.

We spent that evening and most of the next day visiting

Erica at her apartment. We talked about her plans and updated her on how we were doing. We don't see her nearly as often as we would like, prohibited mainly by the distance. From Boston, we drove north to visit with friends, the Springers. We brought our new summer drink, basil rum and lemonade. They always have everything set up just right, the snacks and the dining table. We had an early dinner and just spent time chatting. These are two terrific friends.

The next evening, we organized a dinner with some of our closest friends whom we affectionately call "Pew Partners" from our home church in Boston. Most of them served on the Trustee or Steward Board. For whatever reason, we all tended to sit in the same church section every Sunday and constantly commented on the church. It was great to see all of them but not so great to hear how the church managed a major financial disaster.

The next day, we drove to Newport, Rhode Island. We rented a quaint and adequate Airbnb apartment in an old colonial home. The location was perfect, right off Thames Street, in the heart of restaurants and shops. That evening, we ate at one of our usual places, Scales. Attending the Newport Jazz Festival (NJF) was something I loved to do almost every year.

The weather was perfect, meaning plenty of sun, hot but tolerable, and no rain. This was a treat. One of the highlights was Tia Fuller. She was fabulous as always, great sax, and this time, she sang and did spoken word. She played music from her latest recording, *Diamond Cut*. Of all the acts on the stage, she was the must-see and I was satisfied. We then picked up and moved to the Main Stage area to hear Thunder Kat followed by Herbie Hancock. The former I had not heard before. The best way to describe it was "interesting," but not really my preference. The latter, of course, is always great. He had a slamming band and played some familiar songs and other stuff. The day was long but thoroughly enjoyable.

On day two of NJF, we heard Ralph Peterson and the Messenger Legacy (all former Art Blakey Jazz Messengers.) The performance was exceptional, including some traditional post-bop music. Then we were treated to a little Memphis sound with Dee Dee Bridgewater. I was expecting her with a big band, but instead, it was an afternoon of familiar songs. She puts on a great show and can sing! We left early to get some rest and change clothes before heading out for dinner. But before we did, we took a group selfie with Lori Dow, the singer, at my 60th birthday party. The evening ended with dinner at a friend's house in Newport. Everyone should, in their lifetime, spend a day at this grand festival.

It was now time to start our drive back home with several stops. Sunday was our day driving to Connecticut to see friends for a dinner that we arranged. We went to the home of Winston Johnson, drummer in the Quintessence band, and his wife, Cynthia, in So. Windsor. We leisurely spent the afternoon chatting and then dressed for dinner. We met up with other UConn friends and my cousins, Marlene and Darryl Harris, at dinner. The occasion brought several members of Quintessence together. It was nice seeing everyone and sharing old memories. Getting a group of people together is always fun.

The next destination was Catonsville, Maryland, to my mother's apartment. Spending time with Mom is all about making sure she's okay and discussing her plans. We spent the night at LaMonde's. We just chilled before going to bed early after a glass of wine, and we were up the following day to get back on the road.

The final leg of the trip was the drive from Maryland to Charlotte. Riding in the car for that many hours was good for talking about things! Unfortunately, this also included listening to news stories about our government, particularly President Trump. There were two major mass shootings. We switched radio shows between smooth jazz, "real" jazz, soul jams, and old classic radio. We got to contemplate the world, all we have, and all we want to do. I'm better when driving. When Pam takes over, I tend to fall asleep.

On January 23, 2019, we flew to Florida and had time to visit with Bruce and Mary. It was great to see them (and the new dog). Most of the time, we talked and drove around the area. Two days later, Pam and I were on the Blue Note at Sea Jazz Cruise. This was amazing. Daily performances, beginning in the afternoon to after midnight. I got to see people I listen to and others that were new talent. The best act was Marcus Miller, while the most entertaining was Nikki Harris, and Alonzo Bodden was exceptionally funny. And the special treat was to hear Alex Han live. I sat down with Terrence Blanchard to interview for Fusion at Sunset internet streaming station.

The cruising was good and the food was plentiful. The

cabin was small and needed some upgrades. Glad we booked a room with a balcony. I was able to walk from one end of the ship to the other without the need for a wheelchair. I had plenty of company of persons requiring some assistance. There were many people with wheelchairs, scooters, and walkers on board. It had been a long time since we were on a large ship after years of cruising with Windstar Cruises, a small ship company.

The ports were of little consequence. I got off the ship only once, but Pam did explore Key West and Cozumel. We were able to share this experience with our friends from Charlotte, Monica, Elliott, Bill, and Jan. In addition to listening to the music, we would have a meal together or have a cocktail.

In April, we went to Charleston for Pam's birthday.

From My Journal:

Anniversary Week – July 1 - *We drove to Asheville, North Carolina, and stayed for two nights at the Foundry, a new hotel developed in an old steel mill. The room was extra-large, with a great view of the courtyard. We used the car service, a new Tesla with doors that opened upward, to go out for dinner. The first night we ate at Storm Rhum Bar and Bistro. The food was excellent, and so was the rum (Smith & Cross from Jamaica). The second night we ate at The Admiral, highly recommended, and again the food was excellent. The place was smaller than I expected and casual. We sat at the bar and got excellent service. Here I became familiar with Uncle Val's gin. It has the scent of citrus.*

We ate and drank our way through Asheville. Because it's hilly, I could not walk around much. But spending time away from our usual day-to-day was special. It was a way to mark the event and express our love after all these years. Hoping we can make it to fifty years.

September 2019 - We traveled to Hilton Head for my 70th birthday. The celebration was more laid-back than usual. We did go out to hear some music at the Jazz Corner, a prevalent group that played jazz, R&B, soul, etc. Hilton Head was lovely; not much to do if you don't play golf or ride a bike, but we went to the beach one day for about three hours. The condo had beach chairs, and we rented an umbrella. The sun was scorching, requiring lots of shade. I was uncertain about going to the beach with my oxygen, but it worked out. On another day, we drove around and found the historic Mitchelville community, a Black community founded during the civil war. They had a church and school and existed for some time, but eventually, people left. It was nice to see the historical site. I hope we get to revisit Hilton Head.

Up to this point, we were fulfilling our plans to travel. Then, 2020 came and we had little choice but to cancel our travel plans due to the global pandemic. When I get a flight, post-2021, it will be less than a two-hour trip. I'm also reluctant to take a cruise but might be persuaded to consider a luxury liner. There have been far too many ships with an outbreak of viruses or bacteria. That leaves travel by car, where we control the environment. By 2022, my resistance could all change.

Maybe we'll be able to travel to Texas to see members of Pam's family or visit Tucson, to see members of my family and some friends who moved there from Boston or places in the deep south or Nashville, Memphis, and Kansas City, where the music and culture are of interest.

There's so much around the world I did not get to see, but I've seen far more than my parents ever saw. I never traveled to South America, Asia, or Australia. I have no interest in Greenland, Iceland, or Antarctica—too cold. I wanted to see more of Europe, travel throughout the African nations and the Middle East. Maybe I'll get to do at least one of these before traveling is no longer possible. So, where is the next adventure?

CHAPTER 9

Keep On Keeping On

EVERY DAY IS A BLESSING.

Ayear after beginning this book, I find myself looking back to see how I've described this period of my life. There have been some great moments, and then there have been other reminders that I'm not getting any younger.

Life gets measured by ups and downs. There are days when you feel great. You have thoughts of reconnecting with people from your past and you have new experiences and opinions about everything you read, see, and discuss.

I can quickly point to four times during the Fourth Quarter when significant changes impacted my life. The first was in 2012 when I stepped down from my position at the community foundation, a job, in all honesty, I was not enjoying. I took the entire summer off to reset my career and find new employment. I needed the time off. No longer required to live in western Massachusetts during the week, unloading the expense of the apartment and being back home with the family was a blessing. In doing so, I was able to think about what I wanted to do next and be open to something different.

The next time was from the end of 2015 to March 2016. I had given my notice to resign from my position at Nurtury with plans to retire. Then, I received an unexpected opportunity to join the faculty at Boston College School of Social Work. I planned to teach in retirement, so why not? The position was ideal, except we were already selling our home in Canton and relocating to Charlotte. How was I going to teach full-time in Boston and live elsewhere? We found temporary apartments in both cities and began our transition to a new life.

The third blessing came in 2018 when I finally entered into full retirement, completed the move to Charlotte, and focused on my health issues. I probably could have renewed for less than the standard three years. Just the thought of living in one place was now possible for us. Neither Pam nor I needed to work. I was no longer flying back and forth twice a month. In the year ahead, we became engaged in Charlotte's social groups and found a new church home. Life was good.

Finally, during the pandemic, we were able to sell our condo in St. Croix. Unloading the property was a massive relief from the bills after deciding to no longer rent and make sure it was ready to list on the market. Having this asset set aside for our retirement is a blessing. We are fortunate that this process took only one year. In the past five years, the island had experienced some economic setbacks. It was uncertain what might happen with the sale during the pandemic.

Counting your blessings helps in so many ways. It is easy to become aggravated over minor things because you believe you have so many battles to fight. You like things the way they are, so change is hard to make adjustments. You might say to someone, don't ask me to do something a different way after doing it one way my whole life. Wake up! The world around you changes. It gets an upgrade and becomes more modern and highly technical. How many of us used video conferencing for our meetings before 2020? Did you even know Zoom existed? You may have had some experience with Facetime. But now it's different. Besides meetings or socializing with friends/family, we are attending fundraising events and conferences, and watching jazz artists live stream a performance. Watching a band play on TV is not the same as being in a nightclub, feeling the vibe, witnessing the spontaneity, hearing the audience's reactions, and clinking glasses. I miss going to the club or concerts.

From My Journal:

November 2019 - *Fortunately, going out to hear music or dinner still exists. This weekend, we went out to hear music three days/night in a row. I'm not sure I have ever done that before. Pam and I are regular participants at The Jazz Room. The shows are done by Jazz Arts Charlotte, a nonprofit that offers education for youth and monthly performances. This Friday, we went to hear Vanessa Ferguson, who sang Nina Simone. She was good, lots of presence and command of the stage, and lives in NC. Saturday, we went out to hear pianist phenom, Joey Alexander. He had drummer, Kendrick Scott, and bassist Kris Nunn.*

The show was at the new jazz club located in Charlotte, called the Middle C Jazz. The club has been open for one month and doing good business. I have been waiting for a place like this to open in Charlotte. I'm hoping it will continue to bring in national acts and not lean too heavily on local or regional talent. The room looks and feels good—great sound and acoustics.

Then, Sunday, we attended a jazz vesper at St. Luke's MBC performed by the Sign of the Times group. The band performs all over the city. Music is alive in Charlotte, and the jazz scene has stepped up!

When we first moved to Charlotte, there were only a few places to go and not really one decent club per se to listen to jazz. There were concerts, mostly smooth jazz artists, the shows produced by Jazz Arts Charlotte, and the Bechtler Museum with Ziad Rabie's band. But in the past year, there are more concerts and a new venue.

Another activity during the Fourth Quarter is making new connections that can surprisingly lead you to an old connection. Funny, but sometimes sad, how the world works and the relationships we have intersect. This year, I decided to attend a few Charlotte Social Connection (CSC) luncheons. The group of mature Black men gather for lunch once a month to eat and talk, and not much more. There's no specific plan of conversation, just the usual things Black men discuss. CSC has existed for over sixteen years. I have only been to a few of these, but at my second one, I talked to a gentleman named John, who happened to be from Connecticut, and learned we knew a few of the same people. One of those people was Willie from my hometown of Stamford. Willie was one grade level below me in high school. John said Willie lived in Charlotte now, and I indicated an interest in re-connecting. Unfortunately, the phone numbers John provided did not work, and I never reached him.

Weeks later, John told me that Willie passed away and a memorial service had already been held. The story was sad because he had recently put his mother in a nursing home. The nursing home sent the police to his house because Willie had not visited his mother in a while. They found him dead in his home. Not sure how long he had been there. The obituary in the paper was very brief, as if the person writing it knew little about him. There was no mention of a wife or children, only his mother. It referenced cousins but not by name. I wondered if he had family, friends, or work colleagues. It was sad for me to see this, knowing I might have reconnected with him before this tragic event.

It's comforting to know I have family and friends in my life. As they say, nothing is promised. You just don't know when your time to leave this earth will come. Better to stay connected to the people you care for the most.

From My Journal:

This weekend I checked in to see how my mentor Hubie was doing. When you're in this phase of life, it's essential to check to see how people you know and care about are doing. I would want people I mentored to check on me. You worry about being forgotten and just fade away into dust. I had not talked to or heard from him, so I reconnected via email.

Hubie's reply updated me on his and Kathy's health and the work with Higher Ground. I'm not sure of Hubie's age, but I do know it's north of 80. One afternoon, when we were heading out for lunch to discuss my employment plans, I asked him, "How do you keep it going?" His simple reply was, "Keep moving." He has reduced his community activity to give more attention to his wife's needs. There was a follow-up exchange that updated me on his son. He further wrote, "I have helpful support, focusing me on living in the present because I cannot control the future. Kathy and I live robustly: going to concerts, theatre, public events, and dinners with friends. We are having a good time in the present."

A Great Day in Boston: (left to right) Mel King, Hubie Jones, Karilyn Crockett, Greg T. Ricks, and me. (2012)

Hubie is well into his Fourth Quarter and endures many challenges. The fact that he continues to stay engaged at his age is remarkable. He has been one of my biggest supporters and an inspiration as I seek to be involved in the community while retired. Hubie has given more than most to the community, and the community should be giving back to him. Hubie works tirelessly on many fronts. We should all be as committed to helping our community.

During the Fourth Quarter, you are wise to have all your stuff in order. Not only have a legal will, but a clear plan for what you want to happen after you die. Reach out and connect to everyone you care about, especially if you have not talked with them or seen them in decades. Decide what you want your family to do with the items you leave behind. For me, I'm perplexed trying to figure out what to do with my collection of vinyl albums, CDs, compositions, and tape recordings. Decide on your legacy, and if possible, make a charitable gift to some organization. It's not enough to organize your life while in retirement, but recognize life can change. You may last for another twenty years, or it could be a lot shorter. Whatever the length of time, enjoy the moments and stay as active as you can.

The Fourth Quarter is a period in your life, unfortunately, when you'll increasingly experience the loss of friends and family members. These are the family members who cared for you when you were a child. Sometimes it's a friend from school or a younger person who mysteriously fell victim to an unknown or unexpected illness. Whenever I visited my Uncle Donnie, he would tell me about a person from our hometown who passed away. Most of the time, I had no idea who he meant. Regularly, he read the daily hometown newspaper, especially the obituary section. Now I understand why.

From My Journal:

I learned that a colleague, one of the people who helped start the New England Consortium of Black Admissions Counselors (NECBAC), passed away. During those years, she worked at Tufts. She and her family lived in the Chicago area. Later in the week, we learned that the husband of one of the students I enrolled at UMass Boston, with whom I stayed in contact, had passed away.

Another friend from high school was leaving on a cruise but became ill with pneumonia type symptoms and died in a few days. Not sure if this was one of the early COVID-19 deaths. A year before, we were having lunch and reminiscing about the old days.

We have lost several family members since we have been in Charlotte. For many of our friends, a husband or wife, sister or brother, aunt or uncle, cousins, high school, or a military buddy have died. It's all around us.

Our family was shocked by the news that a nephew passed. Not sure what he was doing in the overnight hours, but his wife and sons could not revive him. None of us expected it given his age. He lived in Vermont, so we rarely got to see them but on occasion, he would call.

Calvin, Jr., Pam's brother, also passed away. He lived in the eastern part of North Carolina with his wife. Calvin had been battling several health issues and then lost the fight one day. He has three daughters, who all live in other states, not nearby, and took his passing very hard.

We watched Phyllis's journey. Things were generally okay until one day, Phyllis fell at the apartment and could not get out of bed for a couple of weeks. At one point, we thought we were losing her, but to our surprise, she recovered. A niece, her friends from Raleigh, and her new church friends, all came by to visit. It must have been the collective prayers that kept her with us. Her pain was increasing and becoming unbearable. Pam went over to see her every day to help relieve the pain and provide care. Like most of us, she did not want to go to the hospital. Caring for a family member feels like a sacred obligation, a responsibility, something you must do.

On April 8, 2020, around 6:30 AM, Phyllis passed away. On the advice of the hospice care worker, Pam had spent the night expecting that she had only one to two days. I believe her final moment was peaceful. Thank goodness she had a great core of buddies from churches in Charlotte and Raleigh.

RIP Phyllis. Say hello to David and Tim.

CHAPTER 10

Faith and God

"TRUST IN THE LORD WITH ALL YOUR HEART AND LEAN NOT ON YOUR OWN
UNDERSTANDING; IN ALL YOUR WAYS SUBMIT TO HIM AND HE WILL MAKE YOUR
PATHS STRAIGHT."
-PROVERBS 3:5-6 NIV

I believe there are four things you must do in life that make it possible to say you are a good person. 1) Work hard and smart. Whatever you do, be the best at it. We must all contribute to the greater society. 2) Be kind and generous to your family, friends, and community. Refrain from negative comments or thoughts about other people and instead, offer to lend a helping hand to those in need. 3) Adopt a set of principles and values to guide your actions. Check your ego and function with the highest level of integrity. 4) Praise God for all He has done and will do. Recognize that you could not do what you do without Him.

I was raised in a Christian household and have ministers in my family (uncles and aunts on my mother's side). I grew up attending church, saying my prayers at bedtime, and reciting a short verse as a child. I love gospel music. As a young adult, I did not attend church regularly. But, somehow, He knows you will find your way back to some form of religious practice or develop a spiritual belief.

By the time I was fifty, I had realized that God predetermined my steps. I would decide my journey, but ultimately, I was there to do His work. Even when the job did not go as well as expected, there was still a purpose greater than I could see or understand. Things did not go as expected in western Massachusetts. I knew it was not a place where I felt good about the work and realized it was not a good fit. *Did God want me to be there? Was I failing Him? Was I having the impact the organization needed, but I could not see it?* I can point to several things I believe were accomplished. I also recognize that this was when I was inducted into Sigma Pi Phi, a fraternal membership. In any case, I left that position and returned home to Boston to find a new and more fulfilling job. I share this brief story to say, life is not always what you want or expect it to be, but your faith will protect you and see you through the trials and tribulations.

Now that we live in Charlotte, we searched for a new church home. Charlotte is the headquarters for the A.M.E Zion Church, yet we decided to seek a Baptist church before looking at other protestant churches since Pam grew up in a Baptist church. After months of visiting a few houses of worship, we found a home at Friendship Missionary Baptist Church, a well-known megachurch in the city. But going to church is the easy part.

It has not been that easy to get involved in one or more of the multitude of ministries. I eventually got engaged as a volunteer at Friendship Day School while Pam found her calling to join a national Bible Study Fellowship program, where she connected with other Friendship members. We later discovered that some of our friends from various social groups attend FMBC. We enjoy the splendid music and sermons. Although we have not become fully engaged in a ministry, there are plenty to choose from if one is so inclined.

How do we go through each day as a Christian and a believer in Jesus Christ? What does it mean to be a believer? How do you express that to non-Christians so they can understand? Belief in God and Christ is personal and hard to explain. I'm not one to preach to others about God and Christ, but I can testify that He has helped bring me through my issues. Clearly, I would not be able to live with this disease without my faith.

From My Journal:

Church Closed for Easter (4-13-20) - *Who would ever imagine churches being closed on Easter? It took a pandemic to shutter services on the holiest day of the year. Pam and I watched our Pastor deliver a sermon via online streaming. The subject was "Bringing Light into Darkness." How appropriate. At 11 AM, we wished Mom a happy 89th birthday, all still in lockdown. So, where is the message from God? Is this the equalizer or is it a wakeup call for something bigger that's yet to come? What is certain is that things will be different, and we must be ready. Erica arranged a conference call with LaMonde and Nicole, Chris and Danielle with baby Naomi, and Pam, and me. There were many blessings shared among friends wishing each other a happy Easter. It was a quiet and somber day.*

A Prayer (5-17-20) - God is good! This week, I received a surprise deposit in our savings account. It was a check from SSA that was not expected and made me nervous. I had to call them to determine if it was related to an appeal requested a few years ago. In any case, it was a welcomed boost. So, I said a little prayer to thank you, God. They say, He steps in right on time.

Not too long ago, we also received word that we have a buyer for our condo in STX. We just listed the property in March but fully expected the sale might take time due to the coronavirus. Maybe it took longer, but we had an offer after seven weeks. The plan is to close the sale by the end of May. This financial good news came when so many people are facing major setbacks due to the pandemic.

But not so fast. The purchase fell through because the buyer could not put together the financing. I should never forget not to celebrate until it's over. This sale went into overtime. Regardless, thank you, Lord, for all you have done for Pam and me. Thank you for the feeling of recovery after a few days of struggling with breathing and feeling very weak. I pray my health continues to get better. I know there is no cure, but being able to walk, exercise, and enjoy social activities is a blessing.

I pray for school children who could not finish school this year. I pray healthcare workers can work and be safe. I pray the government puts aside politics and does what's right to everyone safe. I pray those who are unemployed can find work. I'm hopeful that the economy improves and small business owners can revive their businesses. I worry about an increase in crime and mental health problems. These are difficult times and the most uncertain.

God continues to look out for Pam and me as we try to help loved ones and others. Amen

Through these difficult times, you must have faith and hope. Trust your belief in Him, and He will provide what we need, even though it may not be what we want. I hope there will be a brighter day ahead. Faith that our leaders turn away from all the evil actions and realize it's tearing this world apart. Hope, for all the hopeless who cannot speak for themselves, that others speak up on their behalf. I have always wondered whether we are born evil or become evil. In either case, we need to be saved from ourselves. There is just too much hate in this world.

This year, we attended worship via online streaming. I would never have imagined listening to a sermon on my iPad like the elderly viewing television evangelists. I miss sitting in the pew and watching other people, the feeling you get from the music, or the moment when the Spirit fills the sanctuary. Of course, the greetings and comforting hugs you receive during the fellowship before and after service. I'm looking forward to returning to the weekly ritual of attending church, getting out of bed, eating breakfast, and dressing up to find a good parking spot along the side of the building. What a feeling that will be.

My faith is strong when you have others around you who

also have faith. They tend to pray for your recovery and ask Him to give you strength, comfort you, or ease the suffering. I rise in the morning and start a new day, knowing that He is there with me. I don't know where the journey from here will take me but I pray I'm not a burden to Pam. That I will not linger around, requiring a lengthy need for personal care. I hope I have time to say goodbye to the people I care about, and I have time to leave behind any last wishes. I have expressed to Pam to get help from friends, family, or healthcare workers through an agency when it's too much for her to manage. It can become more work than any one person can handle.

Chapter 11

Staying Active

People hesitate to retire because they have difficulty figuring out what to do with extra time. When you're working, like most folks, you spend more than a 40-hour week on the job, plus all the other things you do around the house and with friends. If you're married, you have the usual honey-do list. Trust me, that list does not go away but can be different. There are meetings, community service, church, etc. As I look back on those days before retirement, I can't believe I found time to do everything I did. Beyond getting one thing done each day, I have free will to do whatever I choose, including sitting on the deck with a beverage in hand and listening to nature or jazz. I can honestly say I'm enjoying not having to get up in the morning to go to work and all that comes with the day.

As I have said, I organize and must plan almost everything. I rarely leave my calendar open with nothing to do, which led to me create a retirement list where I check off what I complete. I can honestly say after two years, I have achieved very little. Yet, I have been socially more active now than ever before. I had replaced work with socializing before the pandemic took over our lives. Most men have the usual list of home improvement projects, fix this or replace that. We did some of that in 2019 into the beginning of 2020. But as retirees, we instead hired someone to get it done. In general, I consider myself a handyman, but the projects were more work than I should and could do at this stage of life.

The primary objective was not to get sedentary. I must keep moving, as Hubie told me. Do not settle into a recliner. I don't golf like many of my friends or swim in a pool at the YMCA. I'm no longer able to go for a long walk. I find myself sitting a lot, working on projects that keep my mind active but not the body. This chapter discusses four of those activities.

Music Recordings - I had planned to digitize most of my vinyl album collection and then find a place to sell or donate them. I learned that digitizing was a much greater task than I imagined. The vinyl collection is about 650 albums. It includes jazz, R&B, and gospel, with a few other items thrown in. The realization is, to digitize each album, you must fully play them. It takes too many hours and days. Needless to say, this was not going to work. In addition to the vinyl, I have hundreds of CDs. Combined, I have over 1200 vinyl albums and CDs.

I have found a few places that buy and sell old records, but the clerks have limited knowledge of jazz. They don't recognize some of the best stuff and won't buy it. What am I to do with all this music so it won't end up in the dump? I need to find time to address my albums and my music. It will make me feel a lot better knowing I did not leave it behind for someone else to manage or toss away.

Also, I have sheet music with the songs I have written, cassette tapes of the band performing a concert, and reel-to-reel tapes from the recording studio. I absolutely can't throw these gems away! My dream would be to create a songbook of my compositions for some musicians to one day play. How sweet would that be? Like everything else, I must put out the effort (time) to get it done. I believe I have the time, not necessarily the energy.

I envision an extensive archival library of jazz recordings and I have found two places where this idea exists. One place is the ARChive of Contemporary Music in New York. In 2016, I donated close to 250 recordings. The other is possibly the new American Jazz Museum in Kansas City. Then there are the numerous colleges and universities with some collections but they are usually very selective.

Most of my friends who keep and maintain albums do so out of the love of jazz or other popular music. Albums rarely have much value, but there is the thrill of having a vast number of recordings in your possession. A few of us might have plans for what should happen in our estate plans. I have been trying to address this before it's too late. So far, I have started a collection listing using Discogs that provides a complete accounting of my collection.

Ancestry/photos – Do you ever wonder where your ancestors come from? Like many people, I spend many days searching for my family history using Ancestry.com. I get all revved up and spend hours for about two days, hit a wall, and then let it rest for months. I have also participated in the DNA testing that shows 80% of my family's origins are from Western Africa.

The Fourth Quarter has been great for conducting ancestry research and organizing photos. Pam and I attended a workshop to help us create a legacy by moving photos from print and scanning them to create a digital file. Between all our pictures and the pictures from our mothers, Pam and I have a large number of photos of us and most of the family members going back to when our parents were young.

I also became more curious about the name Ancrum and my roots from Orangeburg, South Carolina. I had some information to start me on this journey to learn more. In 1979, I received a letter from L. F. Gebbett, a person from London researching the Ancrum family and descendant of Michael Ancrum (who died in 1762), a merchant in Edinburgh and Wilmington, North Carolina. Gebbett had traced the immigration from Scotland to the new world.

What plantation were my ancestors being held as slaves, and where did they live after the Civil War? Why the current interest? Being in Charlotte, means I live only a one-day trip away from Orangeburg. Wouldn't it be nice to talk with a member of the Ancrum family who stayed in South Carolina? I vaguely remember visiting Orangeburg with my grandmother when I was young. I can recall sitting on the fence at a farm, looking at the pigs with a BB gun. But not much more than that. The best way for me to learn more about the Ancrum family would be to talk with a relative from Orangeburg who can share the stories of their grandparents. I did find one story of a man named Frank Ancrum, probably a cousin two generations back. He was the son of Matilda, a daughter of Rena, living in Holly Hill. Surprisingly, he listed his father's name as Joseph Cain on his death certificate. He worked as a blacksmith and died in 1935 because of a nail in the leg while shoeing a horse. (I find it hard to believe a skilled laborer would injure himself that way.) Then there's William, another child of Rena who died at age 55 in 1931 from accidental drowning when he fell in the water while fishing on a boat. If he could not swim, it makes you wonder why he was out on the water fishing.

I am a descendant of George Emonei Carter on my mother's side. He was born in Prince County, Maryland, was a teacher, became a CMEC minister, educator, wrote for the Negro World and worked with the Universal Negro Improvement Association (or referred to as the Marcus Garvey movement). His book, *Children of Folly*, is housed at the Schomburg Center for Research in Black Culture.

In 1924, there's a photo of him in front of the Negro World headquarters at 54-56 West 135th Street in Harlem, with delegates of the 1924 Fourth International Convention of the Negro Peoples of the World with signatures petitioning President Calvin Coolidge for "a sympathetic consideration of the plan of a founding nation in Africa (later to be known as Liberia)." He sent a letter to W.E. B Dubois, among his papers at the University of Massachusetts in Amherst, dated July 10, 1929. It's written on the letterhead of Union Station CMEC in Petersburg, VA, where he describes himself as the Secretary-General of the Booker T. Washington ship under the UNIA, which he served for four years and six months. He did some extraordinary work in his life that I knew nothing about until I did some digging into my ancestry.

There's a well-written and informative newspaper article about G. Emonei Carter, Sr.'s life written by my great aunt Bessie. The poem begins,

I love you, but God loved you best,
I'll miss you, but you wanted to rest,
I'll need you, but only time will tell,
I only know, with your soul, it is well.

Together with his wife, Edna Myrtle (Harper) Armstead, eight children were born (three died at birth or soon after). The article states that the family members left to mourn were my grandmother Gladys, great aunts, Persephone, Myrtle and Bessie, and George's great uncle. He also had two sisters, Mrs. Lottie Mills and Mrs. Carrie Glascow, of which my cousins and I know very little. On Easter morning, 1940, he passed away in Roanoke, Virgina, where the family held its last reunion in 2015.

I wish I spent more time talking with Aunt Bessie. As we learn more about our ancestry, we also uncover a few family mysteries that the adults did not share. I can only imagine the surprise and humor some might bring to light.

My great grandparents, Mother, and Daddy Carter, as they were called, lived in Virginia when my Mom lived with them. Mother Carter later brought my mom to live on the property she inherited from her mother. This land was our forty acres in southern Illinois. There's so much history about the family to learn.

<u>Volunteerism</u> - The Fourth Quarter has also been a time for me to engage with other people as a volunteer. *If you are blessed with talents, wealth, knowledge, time, and the like, it is expected that we use these well to glorify God and benefit others. (Luke 12:48)*

I have volunteered at the Friendship Day School, operated through the church. For the first year, my volunteer work had become a regular bi-monthly meeting with the Director. As time went by, this work had all but ceased to exist. My hope was for the school to grow and build a school building on the church property.

I found it challenging to do the kind of volunteer work I enjoy, using my skills and knowledge to address organizational issues. It should not have been a surprise. I'm new to this community, and they don't know me or my professional background. I am a stranger in a new land here in Charlotte. Under normal circumstances, it takes time to build trust, so I should not expect anyone to accept my word and openly welcome me into their world. I'm sure it would have been much easier in Boston. I decided I did not want to engage in fundraising and I also chose not to seek board service.

I stopped looking for opportunities until The Males Place came along. I presented a workshop on "Making the Right Decision" to the program for Black boys ages twelve to eighteen. I now work with the organization's founder in an advisory capacity to address various organizational and management issues to enable them to grow and raise funds. I'm hopeful my relationship with the organization continues for at least a year. Organizations involving Black men working directly with Black boys are the best solution for improving the lives of these future Black men. It provides positive role models, teaches them to be respectful, know and learn their cultural history, set education and work goals, and stay away from harmful elements surrounding them.

Watching TV - Pam and I have always watched a fair amount of television. We routinely catch the morning news with a cup of coffee or a light breakfast. After 9 AM, we might continue with a local program or the Today Show or switch to get the sports news and check to see the scores from the day before. If I watch ESPN, I spend part of the time yelling back at Stephen A. Smith, who always yells about something. I miss watching Celtics and Patriot games in this market, but I get enough with the Panthers and Hornets. My sports watching has increased compared to just ten years ago but I love it.

Watching TV is not healthy for many reasons, but it has provided another topic for our friends to discuss during the pandemic. We trade information about our favorite series or send information about an upcoming show via text or email. *Did you see this?* or *Are you planning to watch that?*

The most essential evening program is Jeopardy, which has been a family staple. We will miss Alex Trebek, who passed away. Jeopardy tests your mental muscle, and you always learn something, although it can be just trivia. Television shows at primetime can vary. Most of the network shows are not that good. We don't enjoy all the comedy programs and may watch a few reality shows focused on music or dance. Sometimes we have a favorite or two, mostly a suspense program, involving a mystery or crime theme. As a result, I spend probably six to eight hours per day in front of the television, more time than I need. I try to exercise while watching, using free weights in rare moments. Most of the time, I fall asleep watching and need to rewind the show to see what I missed. Of course, I should be reading a book instead. I have plenty at home and on my list, but I tend not to be in the mood for a book.

During retirement (especially through the pandemic), I have seen many movies and series on Prime and Netflix. I'll have two to three series going on at the same time. Watching television on HBO, Showtime, and Starz began with *The Wire*, my all-time favorite (along with *Lost)*. I have watched the *Game of Thrones* series twice. I can hardly wait for the new prequel to begin. Now there's a massive selection of shows, past and new, to choose from.

Given what we witnessed during 2020, I expect the movie theater industry to slow down and possibly shatter. Why go there when you can stay at home, in comfort, not rush out the door to get a seat and pay lots of money for tickets and refreshments? Now I can start to watch whenever I want, pick my refreshments with my favorite beverage, pause when I need a bathroom break, rewind when my hearing is impaired, or I dozed off for a minute. Even more, I can watch it again and again. Paying a monthly streaming fee is still a savings. How can a typical movie theater compete with these benefits?

Watching so much TV, I've noticed significant changes in programming. For instance, have you noticed the changes in commercials and shows regarding diversity? There are more people of color, mixed-raced families, and LGBTQ+ people represented. Has it flipped so much that white people feel like we did? Has the majority race begun to feel like a minority? The world is changing, but it's not being embraced by all.

The bottom line is to stay active, meaning more physical and mental activity than I have exhibited thus far. My excuse is my health. When we first moved here, I was able to walk for twenty minutes on a treadmill. Now I use a recumbent bike to get my legs moving and heart pumping. When it comes to the brain, I engage with other people, sometimes play an online game, and writing this book keeps me busy but not physically moving. None of the things I do are suitable for my physical health.

CHAPTER 12

Sidelines: Part Two

SOMETIMES THINGS DON'T GO AS PLANNED.

L eading into 2020, we expected a great year of travel, finally selling the condo, continuing to develop new relationships, and reconnecting with old friends. But the central issue has been coronavirus, also called COVID-19. It reared its ugly head in China and then spread worldwide.

Initially, in the US, the state of Washington was the center of most of the outbreaks. But there were other cases where people had traveled from Italy and China to the US's east coast. When these reports first came out, there were no reported cases in our area. The most significant impact to us was the trip we had planned for June to Paris and Amsterdam. We had also planned a jazz cruise for January 2021, which was cancelled. Between school closings, events being cancelled, and travel restrictions, it was a hell of a year. DAMN! In retrospect, this was just the beginning. We did not know how horrible this would become.

From My Journal:

March 2020 - *Alan came to visit. It was a busy weekend filled with lots to do. Last night, we went to the Hornets game, which they won for a change. They played against Houston without Westbrook. After the game, Pam picked us up, and we went out to eat at Noble Smoke.*

The night before, we went out for dinner at Vin & Vino and then to Jazz at the Bechtler Museum. The dinner was great, as always. The music was from the Miles Davis1958 recording, Milesstones, with Coltrane, Adderley, and Red Garland. Ziad, the bandleader, had this young sax player, Sam King, who was phenomenal. He's from Baltimore but attended school in NC, currently jazz studies at NCCU. Keep an eye out for this kid.

March 3 was Super Tuesday. Although we voted early (the Friday before), the election was important. The good news is the results created a two-person race for the Democrats, Biden and Sanders. All the other candidates have now dropped out of the race and support Biden. Warren decided not to support either candidate. These two candidates are alike as well as different. Both are white men, in their late seventies (ages 77 and 78), and are from the Northeast. It is yet to be determined if either will select a female or a person of color as a running mate.

A New Way of Life (3-23-20) - Here we are on March 23. Two weeks have gone by since I started staying home. I'm keeping in touch with family and close friends via email, text, and phone. Pam goes to the grocery store to shop for food and other essential items. The problem is, none of us are sure how long this stay-at-home order will last. The tests, cases, and deaths are still climbing. The feeling is we have not reached our peak in the US, and especially here in Charlotte. When the temps warm up again, and there's no rain, at least I can chill on the backyard deck.

So, what does this mean for our retirement funds? Investments took a deep dive. So has all the income we gained been lost? We have a phone conversation soon with our advisor but not sure what to expect there. At the same time, the kitchen and bathroom renovation projects are costing us and have used up some of our savings. If I only saw this coming. Fortunately, we'll recoup funds from our canceled vacations in June, and our condo has a tenant, as we have the unit listed for sale. Somehow, we should financially make it through all this. I worry but we are not dealing with the financial crisis others must face.

Life will be different. Does this mean more dependence on technology, less socializing, or putting funds aside that are not affected by the economic market? With so many unemployed folks, how will America respond? Plus, a presidential election is happening this fall.

Keep the faith!

Stay at Home (3-26-20) - *Today, we are under the first day of the stay-at-home order by Mecklenburg County. As of yesterday, we had 204 cases. What does this mean? Most things are closed, but essential stores and businesses are open. Of course, we can shop for groceries. Staying home will not be much of a change for me. I have been staying home since March 8, except for attending doctor's visits and dinner on March 13. The order stands until April 16, three weeks away.*

We were very optimistic then.

Politically, Trump was more concerned about getting re-elected than he was about people. He was more concerned that businesses got back on their feet than securing our healthcare delivery. His priorities were in the wrong place, making his usual false statements. By the time we come out of this, our state of affairs will be so bad it will compare to World War II and the Great Depression. We will be recovering from this for the next few years.

How does a person with his wealth and position understand what the average person in America needs? Trump was too far removed from the rest of us. He and his cronies sought nothing more than power and control. The fight between conservatives and progressives in Congress depends on who has control. The elections in 2018 were important because Democrats took control of the House that slowed down the passage of a new bill, or protected existing laws.

But when it comes to public health, how do you pick sides over ensuring all Americans are protected? The wearing or not wearing a mask became political, so was the closing of schools and businesses. That should not have happened.

From My Journal:

The Reopening of America Begins (5-12-20) – So we thought. After weeks of staying at home, North Carolina joins other states in lessening orders. I'm going to continue staying at home. I don't need to go to work or any other event. Churches have not been given the okay for group worship. Besides eating out, I have no compelling reason to be among the crowd of people.

When we go anywhere, I wear a mask and keep some distance between myself and the next person. This is not over, but there's an urgency to get back to normal. NC has some testing kits, but not enough for everyone.

Uncertainty (6-6-20) - The best way to describe my feelings is through the word "uncertainty." This can apply to so much of what's going on in my personal life and the world.

Life is a daily dose of uncertainties. We're never exactly sure what each day will bring. I might have a list of things, but something else intercedes or disrupts it. It could be good or bad but unexpected. I never could imagine that I would spend four months not getting together with friends. Before this, Pam and I had a very active social life with an assortment of new friends. All that has stopped, at least temporarily, yet we're uncertain when it will return.

Can Hardly Wait (7-7-20) - The New York Times asked what people are looking forward to when the pandemic is over. Most people said, go out to eat at a restaurant, go to the movies, watch a pro sports team, or hang out at a friend's house. Going out to eat is possible in a few places. On June 26, our wedding anniversary, we went to Port City Club. We wanted a table on the patio, but that did not happen. I already decided not to renew Charlotte Hornet tickets. From the list, hanging out with friends is likely. Right now, we would do it in small numbers on our deck and in the backyard.

Not on the list were things like air travel, which was ruled out indefinitely. Related to that is staying at a hotel. We have reservations for this weekend when we go to Raleigh. I am interested in renting an RV for vacation travel but Pam was not interested in that idea. Middle C Jazz Club has re-opened, but I'm not ready for that either. Not sure if Charlotte Jazz Buzz will meet in person this year. Right now, we have gone virtual, like everything else. Not sure when the church will be open either. Pam would like to feel more comfortable shopping in a regular store (beyond groceries) or other theater events.

I found myself thinking about what I was doing and what I wanted to do post-pandemic. I realize that I'm in the waiting place. Dr. Seuss writes,

> *"Waiting for a train to go or a bus to come,*
> *or a plane to go or the mail to come,*
> *or the rain to go or the phone to ring,*
> *or the snow to snow or waiting around for a Yes or No,*
> *or waiting for their hair to grow.*
> *Everyone is just waiting."*

It's not the long lines at the store to pay for the purchase or the "on hold" phone call to speak with the customer rep to resolve a matter. It's not a traffic jam on I-95 around New York City or D.C. or sitting in the doctor's office waiting for twenty minutes to be seen by the doctor for a five to ten-minute consultation. Nope, none of that. I can do that now.

I have books to read, music to listen to, TV programs and movies to watch, and food (plenty of snacks) to eat—plenty of solitude. Our home is ideal for letting the minutes tick away without a care in the world. The wild animal activity scampering and flittering around the yard is more than sufficient. Pam and I discuss all the latest news and humorous quips shared via social media. There is so much going on globally, and with people we know to have us talking for hours on end.

But it's the human interaction that I can't replicate via Zoom or FaceTime. The conversation, the sense of body language and facial expressions. The in-person touch or embrace may go away to avoid a virus's future spread. I miss socializing with my friends, dinner out as a group, listening to music at the club, sitting in the stands at a Celtics game, or sharing wines at a club gathering. I miss the travel to distant places via air or on a cruise ship to visit foreign lands.

We are all in the waiting place for the moment.

From My Journal:

Mostly Staying at Home (8-9-20) - *It has been five months since I started staying at home to protect myself from the coronavirus. I get up in the morning around 7 AM, early for a person not going to work. The coffee is brewed. I have breakfast and watch the morning news. I read the NYT briefs online, Charlotte Agenda, or Qcitymetro, a Black community online newsletter. I move into the home office to work on a few items listed for the day on the phone calendar and stop around noon, have lunch, and relax a little. I might go back into the office but break to watch a movie or episode of some series. By this time, Pam is fixing dinner, eating, watching Jeopardy, more TV, and bed by 10 PM. Occasionally, we go out for essential items, groceries, pharmacies, doctors, stores. Often Pam goes by herself. No church, no dinners with friends, no jazz clubs, the book club for Pam and CJB are virtual. When will this get back to what we did before?*

Am I overly cautious? I don't think so. But I need to do more than sit on the deck and ride in the car. Most of us are tired of Zoom and need better human interaction. I need to find some day trips that are safe and fun.

<u>On the edge of 71 (9-5-20)</u> - Monday (also Labor Day) will be my 71st birthday. As you can expect, it does not feel like another year has passed, and we are not planning anything big or small. The original plans were to be in New Orleans. This weekend is also the birthday of my friend Elliott, and his wife had planned a surprise celebration in NOLA. On Monday, we invited them and one other couple to come over for some drinks and light refreshments. It will be the first time we will have friends at our home since last February. We will gather outside on the deck and in the backyard.

Christmas 2020 was more subdued than in the past. Fortunately, Erica could fly down, despite the risk, from Boston and spend ten days with us. Because of the pandemic, Pam and I had no plans to go anywhere. Most of the time, we sat around the house, taking it easy. We played dominoes for fun. That large set we had in St. Croix was here with us in Charlotte. We had to review the rules and adjust our abilities and skill level. We also played the card game Uno®, bringing out our cutthroat *competitive nature. We watched a lot of television as usual, including the whole series of Raising Dion. The movie, Ma Rainey,* was just released. *Jeopardy* aired every day at 7 PM, and I watched sports, basketball, and football. Of course, there were gifts. We try to keep it low-key and not go all out with expensive items or many of them. My Santa wishes, since I made it known, came true. I got several pairs of Bomba Socks, compression style, and a LA Dodgers jersey with Robinson #42 on the back.

The night before, we had a family gathering via Zoom. My mom, sister, and kids were all together in Maryland, and we were in Charlotte. There was the usual exchange of text messages wishing our friends and other family members a happy holiday and blessings. It was a time to reflect on being grateful for all that we had and not dwell on the downsides of the year.

From My Journal:

<u>By December 27</u> - in the US, 18 million people have been diagnosed with COVID-19. Over 437,000 have died. The vaccine shots have started this month, but more people will die before the spread slows down. I place the severity of this country on Trump. He failed to respond quickly and with

determination, knowing full well what we were going to face. As a result, we are in a severe crisis.

By the end of the year, only 4.5 million vaccines were administered, far below the 20 million promised by Operation Warp Speed. They fumbled the handoff, not ensuring that plans were in place for local distribution. The distribution has not been well managed, and I sit here wondering if I will receive a shot anytime soon.

The pandemic has provided a moment for connecting with family and reconnecting with your past friends. You can search online for people you worked with to see what they are doing now. I have found that some people I knew have moved as we did, and they are not that far away from where we live now. Send a handwritten note or make a phone call rather than send an email or text message. Post photos of what you're doing so others can see you and know you are doing well. Don't wait for them to reach out to you.

One day very soon, you might find a time to gather with friends you had not seen in more than twenty years. You will be amazed at how much you retain about people in your past. Regardless of the years in between, I find the conversation with them is as deep and rich as if the time was only a year, very fresh in your mind.

CHAPTER 13

Health: Part Three

I OFTEN FEEL TIRED, WEAK AND FRUSTRATED. I HAVE LEARNED TO BE AN ADVOCATE FOR MYSELF, AND MAKE SUGGESTIONS ABOUT THE TREATMENT. WHILE I MAY NOT BE A PHYSICIAN, I KNOW HOW I FEEL, KEEP A RECORD OF THOSE FEELINGS, DOCUMENT WHAT SEEMS TO WORK AND WHAT DOES NOT.

The final section on health covers the Fall of 2019 to the present. In many ways, things are the same—there are good days and bad days. I mostly stay at home and go out to get fresh air and walk a little, mostly out of necessity.

It's been a long medical journey and it's far from over. Unless you have had a similar experience, it's hard to fully grasp how it feels not to be able to breathe. To inhale sufficient air to fill your lungs, and the lungs work hard to push the oxygen into the bloodstream through the heart. When you play sports, you can get out of breath. You have seen the basketball players bend over and grab their shorts or the football players go to the sideline to get something to drink. When you're just walking and need to stop, it feels different. Inhaling and exhaling can be labored for minutes, and you must sit or stand still. Your heart races, your blood pressure increases, and nothing is more important at the moment than getting enough oxygen to breathe calmly and steadily. When you are incapable of going for a one-mile walk, climb a flight of stairs, or any activity that causes some exertion of energy, it can be debilitating.

Treating PAH has improved. Persons diagnosed with this

disease live longer with proper management and working with medical professionals. I have found doctors who express sincere concern and offer excellent explanations and guidance. Compassion is appreciated. The key to management is finding the right medicine, engaging in an adaptive exercise regime, and not get depressed. I share my experience with anyone who has this or a related disease.

From My Journal:

My breathing difficulties were not over. My fourth episode with severe breathing problems was just a year ago, on Oct 30, 2019. Now that I have experience, I self-diagnosed the situation and simply called my doctor to approve a prescription of Prednisone and increase my oxygen level from three to five liters. I stayed at home and away from the hospital. We got it under control and have continued to search for the proper medications at the correct dosage.

Happy New Year/Health (1-1-20) - I depend on air a lot more now at five liters per minute. And yet, I get out of breath quickly and after minimal exertion. After four hours on the portable concentrator, I feel tired. I get these twinges around the heart, not too sharp, but enough to make me wonder what's going on. I will ask my doctor for an EKG to see if that can reveal anything. My stomach is so bloated that I need to fast or go on a strict diet. My feet get swollen, and I sometimes experience a sharp twinge. My hands will cramp, making it difficult to grasp objects, and I'm aware that my hand might tremble when bringing a drink to my mouth. I have not been able to exercise, therefore, my muscle strength is lacking in lifting most things. Overall, I do not feel as good as I would like. I plan to bring all these things up with my doctor on January 9, hoping we can answer some questions.

How am I? Do you ever think about how you respond to people when they ask you "how are you?" Recently, I stopped to think about whether I give an automatic response or tell them how I actually feel. In general, I believe it's an auto-reply, "I'm good" or "Okay," whether I feel that way or not. I quickly return the gesture, if I'm being polite at all, and ask how they are. This is natural.

If I had time to think about it and wanted the person asking to know more, my response would probably take a few minutes. I might tell them what upsets me, that I have a pain in my back, that I'm tired (which is often these days), or something less than positive. Of course, when I feel great, I want them to know that, too. Pam and I know a person, a former leader in Boston who always responded "fabulous." It's a great way to start a conversation with an upbeat and charged reply. I wish I could do that.

I need to take more time to listen to what people say to me and follow that up with an appropriate question to learn more about them or what's going on in their lives. The truth is, the initial response is a precursor to what should follow; therefore, I'm okay is insufficient. There's a commercial on TV that asks, just okay? Why is someone great today or not feeling well? How could I make them feel better? Do I care, or am I trying to move on to talk to someone else? How am I? It should matter, and I need to think more about my response when asked.

Finding a doctor can be challenging. Finding one you like and trusting they have your interest at hand is another matter. You don't always have a positive experience at an appointment. Often you wait for an extended period to see the doctor, and then they spend five minutes with you if you're lucky. My primary care physician and pulmonologist are both personable, thorough, and show genuine interest in my well-being. I feel I'm receiving excellent care from them, and they immediately respond to my issues as they surface.

From My Journal:

March 16, 2020 - I saw the Pulmonary doctor last Monday, and we discussed my PAH. Generally, he seems to be good with where I am. I raised questions regarding Prednisone. On Thursday, I saw a cardiologist recommended by another doctor. As a result, I'm headed back to his office for a right heart de-catheterization test. This test will let us know how things have changed since then, now that I'm using these two prescribed meds. The only thing remaining is to figure out how to get the proper exercise at home.

April 27, 2020 - I cough more, wheezing more, and my nose is constantly running. This could be my allergies. Some parts of the body feel stiff and ache left arm and shoulder area and right above the knees when I rise to get up. I am getting weaker due to absolutely no exercise since October. I feel tired all day. When I sit down, I fall asleep for a few minutes. I wake up tired in the morning, even after going to bed early. A midday nap does not help. I am trying not to burden Pam; she needs a break. I'm refusing to go to the hospital. That would be hell. I will instead be home in bed here.

July 30, 2020 - Yesterday, I had a cardio right-side catheterization test at Novant Medical Center. This appointment was initially scheduled for March but got canceled due to the pandemic. I had this same test done in Dec 2017 in Boston, which determined that I had PAH. The good news is the results were better.

October 15, 2020 - We purchased a recumbent bike, and I hope to use it 3-4 times per week, minimum. When I go into the guest room to watch TV, I must get into the habit of riding the bike and lifting weights for my arms. As much as I can, I should walk more. Going with Pam to the store helps on occasion. We should find a time to walk outside at the park on Hucks Rd. I always watch what I eat, so a diet is not for me. Eating less will help, and reducing my ice cream intake will too. I love ice cream! Getting my weight under control will help me in several ways, currently at 187 pounds.

November 5, 2020 - Last week, I found out I needed cataract surgery. I had been experiencing sight issues, mainly blurring vision. Outside it looked hazy. Watching TV felt like it had a glare screen cover. It has been harder to see from a distance without glasses and to read with glasses. I have an appointment on January 6 for a consultation. Just another thing to take care of in the months ahead.

David Carpenter, entrepreneur and business owner, writes in his article on 60+ years of age, *"even positive life changes can cause our anxiety levels to increase. Humans are creatures of habit. We develop routines that make our lives predictable, and we rely on that predictability to give us comfort."*

We seek to live in relative stability and develop routines to keep us from getting bored or overworked. A major life-changing event will increase your anxiety. I know mine did and still does. I also evaluate myself to determine if I am becoming depressed. At times, I catch myself just sitting in a chair staring into space with what feels like a sad face. I quickly change my expression and notice all the lovely things around me and how wonderful life has been and will continue this way.

You have lots of moments in baseball when the batter is facing a full count, three balls, and two strikes. Unless the next ball pitched is a hit or foul tip, the batter strikes out or walks. The pitcher wants to avoid as many of these as possible, but they usually have a pitch they throw in this situation. They hope the batter will strikeout, hit a line drive, or fly ball into an out. It's probably the game within the game between the pitcher and batter. The batter feels they have the pitcher in a bind and can use this to their advantage to get a hit.

In football, a similar moment repeats itself during a game when the offensive team has a fourth-down situation. The coach must decide whether to punt or run a play to retain possession by moving the football the distance necessary for a first down. The decision is made based on many factors. You consider where the ball is on the field, how well the team has played, and how many inches or yards to get a first down or score. In any case, keeping the ball out of the opposing team's hands is the goal.

Finally, every team hopes to play extreme defense in basketball to keep the other team from scoring before the twenty-four second shot clock runs out of time. Hopefully, the defense is good enough to cause a shot clock violation, and the players are headed back down the court. The other team will get off a shot most of the time, but it might be a prayer shot with no hope of ever going in. That, however, could lead to a rebound by the other team and a second opportunity. Both teams must watch the shot clock to win these little battles.

I'm not sure how many battles you will enter during your life. My most prominent issue, and the one that has gone on the longest, has been my health. I'm looking for a big hit after a full count, or a first down that gives me the advantage or a last second shot that is either rebounded to score some points or continued play.

I was looking for a change in 2021. Getting to a level of stability and comfort with all the issues I'm facing is the goal. With Pam's help, we constantly re-evaluate my situation and the medication treatments by my doctors. No matter what happens, I must stay positive and hope for the best.

Unfortunately, the beginning of 2021 is already a mixed bag of good and bad. The coronavirus spread is not under control. As a matter of fact, the number and percentage of cases peaked higher than before. People have COVID-19 fatigue; some are wearing mask-less frequently and gathered in groups in public, disregarding the contagious nature of this virus. We hear about other strains of the virus from the UK, Brazil, and South Africa that are more contagious and deadly. Will this pandemic ever end?

At least two vaccines are now available, and others are on the way, but the rollout schedule has not kept pace with what was stated by the federal government, and most states' preparation is lacking. As a person over 65 with underlying health issues, I became eligible to get a vaccine and jumped at the first opportunity. Despite getting the vaccine, staying at home is the best defense against getting infected. Maybe later this summer of 2021, depending upon whether the number of positive cases and deaths decreases, I will become more adventuresome to attend a few public events. Going out without the threat of the virus may take until 2022. I pray our country can get on the same page, eliminating the disparity.

Chapter 14

The Unprecedented Year

2020 WILL GO DOWN IN HISTORY AS THE MOST TRAGIC TIME DURING OUR LIVES (MY LIFE FOR SURE). THERE'S NO REASON I CAN THINK OF TO EXPLAIN WHY ALL THIS HAPPENED AT THE SAME TIME, BUT SOME OF IT IS DIRECTLY RELATED.

The most common word used in the news this past year has been "unprecedented." I write about this for two reasons. I'm very concerned about this country, America, and how all this anger and rage will play out. Second, much of it has affected the quality of my life in the Fourth Quarter. After all, this book is about me. This past year has provided lots of time to think about what's going on globally. It has also been time to look at myself. Re-evaluate my situation. Adjust to a new normal.

There have been so many disastrous events affecting public health, the economy, and protests for social justice nationwide, especially the (first) Trump impeachment trial that failed in the Senate. He was acquitted of the charges despite most people's belief he was guilty of poor judgment and involvement.

From My Journal:

Messing with Mother Nature – *Throughout the year, we had the most extensive land fires out west and a continuous barrage of hurricanes and tropical storms. The White House refuses to recognize and acknowledge the impact of climate change on the weather.*

(June 6, 2020) It's uncertain if the economy will recover again. We have gone from very low unemployment to the highest since the last recession. Unfortunately, Black folks, people of color, and low-income households feel the brunt of this pain. The low-paying jobs where these groups tend to be will be the last to return. It is uncertain how this will impact us.

I can't remember when I was so wrapped up in a national election. I consistently exercised my vote but spent more time thinking about the results in Massachusetts and the city of Boston. I got engaged when Mel King had a run at the mayor. I got involved with Ralph Martin's campaign for Suffolk County DA and a limited degree with Duval Patrick's campaign to be MA Governor. Even in 2008, Obama's election to his first term was exciting. The 2020 election was more crucial, in my opinion, because I could not stomach the thought of another four years of Trump. I'm glad Biden was the candidate, and Harris was the running mate. During the period leading up to and after the election, I became obsessed with it and related issues.

From My Journal:

Election - The elections are also upon us. We plan to vote early (next week). I pray that people vote in huge numbers and elect Joe Biden. It's really about voting Trump out of office.

America can no longer have a man like this running our country. There are so many issues of concern. But his constant lies, self-absorbed personality, and disrespect for everyone regardless of their status. He does not care for the average person, just himself.

October 20, 2020 - VOTE! - Yesterday, Pam and I went to vote early. As expected, there was a line, but not too long. In total, it took one hour to stand in line and return to the car. The process was easy, and the people were helpful. We did not witness one incident to tell.

Now I await the voting on Election Day, November 4, 15 days from now. I can't remember a more important election than this. It was exciting to vote for Obama, but it was not following the type of leadership we had these past four years. Trump is a man who has divided this country in more ways than we could have imagined. He's a pathological liar beyond belief. He has done everything possible on policy issues to eliminate what the previous administration had done, not because it was right, just because it was there.

Now Trump has called Dr. Fauci, his medical advisor and specialist on infectious diseases, nasty names. Americans overwhelmingly love this guy and believe in what he tells us. Hopefully, this has cost him more votes. I'm also pulling for Jaime Harrison in SC. He has out-fundraised Lindsey Graham and seems to be on track for a close race. What an upset this would be.

More on VOTE! - Today is Saturday, October 31, Halloween, but more importantly, a few days before Election Day. All of my friends and family are praying that we have a change in the leadership of this country. We have all dreaded the past four years living under an egotistical maniac, serial liar, and perpetrator.

It's hard for me to understand how Trump attracts as much support as he does. The current political climate means this country will be going through a long period divided on issues before we mend the wounds created by this administration. Will Biden/Harris be able to turn this around? Not sure about that, but can they stop the bleeding? I voted early and was clear about selecting Biden or, better yet, anyone other than Trump. Which begs the question, when was the last time you were excited about a candidate for president? Was that Barack Obama? Or was it going back farther? I know I was not excited about my vote for Hillary Clinton, the only choice I had in 2016. There was something about her as a candidate I did not trust. Based on her years of political service, she had plenty of experience. It's hard to ignore your gut feelings.

I should get ready to be more engaged in politics in the next few years, especially at the state level. Last week, I received a flyer that presented a brief outline of the Biden/Harris Agenda for Black America. The circulation was to get more Black people to the polls rather than sitting it out. It tries to communicate that they plan to make things better for Black America. My first reaction to the document only raised three areas of concern, Justice, Health Disparities, and Education. It did not cover all the necessary issues oppressing Black America, and most of what they wrote was the same old shit, very cookie-cutter, and not very innovative. Where are the policy changes to create jobs and decent wages? Where was Bernie Sanders' free tuition for college? Where was affordable housing? The countdown begins, and the campaigns will soon end. Let's get ready to roll up our sleeves and work towards mending this country.

From My Journal:

The Day After - Yesterday was Election Day, and I and all of my friends are hoping for a Biden victory. As of this morning, the presidential race is not over. The final eight states, including NC, are too close to call. All the polls suggested a likely Biden win, but for some reason, Republicans come out on election day and surprise the best of pundits. I'm holding on to a possible win, but it does not feel good at the moment. We might be counting ballots in PA for the next five days.

I'm more worried about the nation divided on issues. In my gut, I feel that politics will worsen before they get better. This could be a rough four years politically. With a majority conservative Supreme Court, previous laws might be changed or wiped out. Race relationships will undoubtedly be at greater odds. Shooting and killing Black men will increase, and justice not served. I am clearly more depressed about this country than ever before.

What's more disturbing is not realizing how many voters support this president. We might have thought he accidentally slipped by Clinton to win, but despite his arrogance, there seems to be an uncanny amount of support. How can Americans like this guy? Put aside his politics and odd behavior alone, he is far from being the kind of president we need to represent America to the rest of the world. I don't feel the economy is better, and the only people to have benefitted from his new tax laws are wealthy households. His handling of the coronavirus is appalling. God help us all.

The 2020 election has been the most stressful yet historical I've experienced. Thank goodness Governor Cooper was re-elected in NC. What should I be doing in the next few years? How can I help in some small way to support the president (Biden) manage his need to bring us, America, closer and work across the divide?

<u>Biden Declared Winner! (11-9-20)</u> - It took five days after the election, but AP projected Biden, the winner, after the states reported the early readings. My friends and other folks who voted for Biden/Harris ticket are celebrating. This election had the largest voter turnout since 1900. It was very close, and few states have yet to release final numbers.

The elections were over in November. Trump never conceded, nor is it required, and he and his supporters hold onto claims of fraud and an election stolen. It's incomprehensible how these lies and false rumors have been sustained, especially why they are perpetuated. He has proven that he cannot live to bear the thought he lost. It makes me wonder whether Trump tried to rig the election but failed.

Maybe he attempted to ensure a win, as he claimed he would win, by initiating some process for cheating.

The world watched in horror at the insurrection of the US Capitol Building on January 6. That day was like no other. It started just fine. I woke up in the morning at the usual time and checked my cell phone for news on the Senate runoff election in Georgia. CNN had already projected a win for Warnock and a slightly favorable edge for Ossoff. We needed these congressmen elected so the Senate would not be a barrier to the Biden agenda. Later that day, a victory was declared, giving the Democrats a 50-50 split in the Senate, with Vice President-elect Harris the tie-breaking vote as Senate president.

I then went to the eye doctor's office for a follow-up after eye surgery. I could now see better with the right eye, but the left eye remained. In his opinion, the operation was successful, and my vision was now at 20/20. I learned that cataract surgery is a standard procedure but is easily correctable with a lens replacement. This was again great news.

Pam and I got home after shopping at the grocery store. I called my Mom to let her know the mail she sent me had arrived. She was all excited to chat about what was going on in the news. It was news to me. We hung up to check the news and our country was under siege by Pro-Trump supporters who stormed the Capitol Building to disrupt Congress. The primary congressional agenda was to certify the Electoral College votes and finally declare Biden/Harris as the president/vice president-elect, paving the way for a January 20 Swearing-in ceremony. This act, storming the building, was in pure defiance of our system and democracy. These individuals were first called protesters, but their actions were that of a mob, rioters, terrorists, and anarchists as the afternoon unfolded. News reports were clearly stating the event was instigated by Trump. He did not immediately condemn their violence or condemn the act of inappropriately entering the symbolic halls of our nation's government which he had sworn to uphold in the constitution.

On January 13, the House of Representatives voted to impeach the president for the second time. The FBI is trying to arrest and bring to the courts as many persons who stormed the building as they can as domestic terrorists. We know that five people, including a Capitol police officer, died. Many police were injured that day, depending upon what report you hear, and the building required extensive repairs. It was a clear threat. Trump should have been held responsible, along with some Republicans who perpetuated the lies and might have provided support and aid to the rioting crowd.

There must be a point at which stating misinformation and promulgating conspiracy theories crosses the line to becoming a criminal act, especially when it is knowingly deliberate. We all believe in free speech, but this speaking out must be brought under control and stopped rather than allowed to grow. When the information can be proven to lack clear evidence of truth, the person responsible for the lie or false statement must be held accountable.

And yet again, there were not enough votes to convict Trump. It isn't easy to know what we can expect in the next four years. Let's pray for brighter days ahead.

Now the real work begins. Both Democrats and Republicans, and maybe there are more than two parties/political platforms, feel strongly on issues that may not be possible. I suspect things might get worse before they get better. I believe the new administration has done whatever it can to control the coronavirus, but ultimately, it's up to the people. Too many still refuse to wear a mask, participate in large gatherings, and not take the necessary precautions to protect themselves. How will people respond if the US needs to order another shutdown for 2-4 weeks because of the new strain?

As we approached 2021, we were all waiting for the vaccine; at that point, the vaccine was still months away, and some had little confidence. I worry about those who will not get the vaccine. Will everyone who wants one has it by the summer, and how effective will it be after six months or against new strains? Despite reassurance from medical experts, many people are skeptical of the vaccine or refuse the shot. Because their small businesses had to close, people were desperate to get back on their feet after losing their savings, home and falling deeper into debt. We can only pray that 2021 will be better than 2020, and with the last election, we are already one step closer.

These last four years are unprecedented because most of us have not been in this kind of mess before. That does not mean that we historically have not had similar incidents in government or dealing with a pandemic before. I can honestly say that I don't always approve of what our government does, but I support democracy.

From My Journal:

Living in America (7-7-20) - *I have begun to think about what it means to be an American. There are so many articles written and news stories that have raised questions about how Blacks have been treated in the US; post-slavery, reparations, Civil War monuments, and taking down Confederate flags. Most of this is symbolic, not just from a historical perspective, but for the racism that has continued after slavery in the form of Jim Crow. It's difficult for me to understand how so-called Americans can still embrace racism from the late 1800s into the early 1900s. It's clear; there are a small percentage of "haves" and a much more significant percentage of "have nots." I have lived in the middle, with some privileges and well enough above poverty to not worry about food, housing, income, etc. But so many of my brothers and sisters live in situations that make it difficult to enjoy the freedoms of being American.*

The BLM movement has caught fire and has spread across the globe. Awareness of history and the parts that have been erased are being revealed. There is a new energy among young people that has not been seen since the 1970s. People have had enough from the extreme far-right and white supremacists that we have few options other than to fight back, even if it means a battle.

One of the bright moments of 2020 was the continued emergence of the Black Lives Matter movement. The fight for equality, social justice, and anti-racism continue. In Charlotte, we had 15 straight days of mostly peaceful demonstrations. The artists painted a colorful street Black Lives Matter mural on the main street (Tryon) in uptown that attracted lots of attention. Of course, actions like this also attracted some negative backlash.

Then we demonstrated our anger when a grand jury did not render an indictment against the cops in Louisville for killing Breonna Taylor. How does a Black woman get shot in her bedroom, and no one is at fault? We know who shot her, and yet there's no justice. There is no apology, no wrongful death responsibility, nothing that justifies her killing. She was in the wrong place. Home? My God! Later we learn the cops went to the wrong address. Her current boyfriend is not the person they were hunting. They broke into the apartment and fired their guns. How does this happen in America?

The world protested against the George Floyd killing, a Black man, by police in Minneapolis, MN. We watched the replay of this tragic event on TV day after day as the cop had his knee pressed on this neck, cutting off air, all because he tried to cash a $20 counterfeit bill. Other than our current president, many people joined in solidarity with the protesters. The jury found the cop guilty of his crime. At the same time, Black and brown men and women continue to be shot by police. It's hard to understand a world like this, where deadly force grants police immunity for prosecution.

I remind myself, that I am blessed to be where I am and to have lived the life I have to this point. Despite my health issues, it has been a life filled with opportunities and rewards. Yet, there are so many more people with so little. Without work, underpaid, without shelter, unable to pay rent, living check to check, and not saving. Attacks against Jewish synagogues, Asians, and transgender men and women occur across this nation. Then you add a justice system and law enforcement that has failed to protect those most in need.

CHAPTER 15

Overtime

IT'S NOT OVER UNTIL THE FAT LADY SINGS. (DAN COOK)

Do not presume the outcome before it's time. I told my friend Bruce I was writing a book about my journey in the Fourth Quarter. He was acutely familiar with the reference as if we were twins. He then replied by telling me he and his golf buddies say, "*The way the fourth quarter is going, I hope there's an overtime.*" Just the thought of having more time or an extension of what previously happened is generally a good thing, especially if you were expecting the worst. In basketball, football, and baseball, overtime has different rules. But the bottom line is you have more time to improve the end.

You play an extra five minutes in basketball if the score is tied after the final buzzer. They will continue to repeat this until a team wins by one point. Sometimes the five minutes can take twenty minutes, with all the timeouts or fouls to a player to stop the clock. At this point, the teams are also playing against the clock. Time is a precious commodity.

In football, there is a ten-minute period. A coin toss determines who goes first. If that team scores, the game is over. It's a process that can bring a quick and disappointing conclusion to a well-fought game. However, if the first team does not score, the other team gets a chance.

Teams tied at the end of nine innings in a baseball game continue playing. The match is a duel between the pitcher and the batter and can become very intense. Usually, by the end of any sporting competition, everyone is exhausted but happy to still be in the game.

So, what will I do differently, especially after a year under various stages of pandemic mandates? My health issues are more challenging, and the world confronts multiple crises that affect people of all races and nationalities. To the degree that I can, staying active is an absolute, not an option.

From My Journal:

Let's face it; aging is challenging. You pray to keep living and enjoying what life has to offer. Although I have done a lot (during my life), I still have dreams or wishes of doing more. At times, I find that I walk into a room with a purpose and then find myself asking what I came for. I'm not having a complete memory breakdown, and it's more about keeping focus. I usually return to where I started and recall what I wanted to do as if I left it there.

I'm not sure when my time on this earth will end, but we must all recognize that moment will come. Rest assured, *Keep On Moving* is not about the end but about how we live our lives during this period. For some, it might be a short and quick period. For others, they continue in relatively stable health past 100 years old.

You know you get old, right? You may not look it, you may

not live as if you're old, but you start to feel it. I recently read an article entitled, "Why I hope to die at 75," written by Ezekiel J. Emanuel, a scientist, and university provost. This is not something your family, or friends for that matter, would ever want to hear you say. He's not giving up, nor would I, though the author raises a good question: how long should anyone live, and when is it long enough? He writes, *"Living too long is also a loss. It renders many of us, if not disabled, then faltering and declining."* When we are no longer creative, contribute to society, and enjoy a productive, active lifestyle, do we lose the will to continue?

Age seventy-five may be somewhat arbitrary, but people need more and more healthcare based on his research. Without question, we all know people who continue to work until they are seventy-five or more. I hear about jazz musicians still performing after age eighty as if they could not find anything else to do simply because that's all they know and love. My mom still looks good and suddenly loves to talk about current events. Behind her relatively healthy appearance, she has a few aches and pains, as expected. I wish she lived in a house with my sister or me. Instead, she enjoys and prefers her independence and does not mind living independently at an assisted living facility. Fortunately, Mom lives near LaMonde, who keeps a close eye on her and tends to most of her requests. Because she has support, it's possible for me not to worry too much. We held a virtual party for her to celebrate her birthday. To my surprise, this was the first birthday party thrown in her honor.

Mr. Emanuel further writes that we become "obsessed with exercising, doing mental puzzles, consuming various juice and protein concoctions, sticking to diets, and popping vitamins and supplements." I can relate to all of these and probably more. Would I feel differently if my health were much better? Is the quality of life worth living after age seventy-five just because we can live longer with all the knowledge we have obtained and medical science to sustain life? Am I living a vibrant life filled with all the excitement I had when younger? Will my mental functions, such as solving puzzles and playing card games, be enough? Or will I become depressed because of my lingering health issues? Regardless, I can honestly say, and the writer makes the inevitable point, that by age seventy-five, you more than likely have lived an entire life. To guarantee enjoyment, you can't just sit around and wait for it to come to you. Instead, you get active doing things, hopefully, things that bring joy and happiness into your mind and heart. With a world facing so many problems yet to be controlled or diminished, the personal battles we face can seem pale in comparison.

I have thought a lot about what I would like to do to make a difference. As Gandhi said, *Be the change you wish to see in the world.* It takes a unique person to change the world or to have such an impact that people around the world notice. I try to make a difference in the immediate world around me by helping an individual or group of people. We all have a vision of what we would like to see. The reality is, I can't be sure if what I see is the right vision or even better than someone else.

I can only hope that I can bring my experience and knowledge together in a manner that can make a difference.

While writing this book, I realize that many of my comments are about the things I dislike going on globally. I evaluate the world by all the negative actions of other people and complain that we do not live in a better world. We can't deny that many people are struggling, and some inflict suffering on others. Now is the time to think differently and adopt a more uplifting perspective, "To inspire and encourage change through action." To look at what a better world could look like through a positive lens and advocate for bringing others along to reach that goal. My theory might sound overly optimistic, and I'm wearing those rose-colored glasses from the '70s, but change does not just happen on its own. So many things have changed for the better. We're still fighting the same issues, and now it feels as though our world is about to explode.

I reflect on what I have done during my life and what I could do going forward. My contributions to date have been to form new organizations that seek to bring about equality. In 1976, two of my colleagues and I developed the idea for a consortium for Black admissions counselors, and it continues to exist today. In 1979, I helped launch a professional development program to help persons of color advance in the college admissions profession. In the 1990s, through the consulting firm, we managed a collective to support Black-led nonprofit organizations serving the Black community in Boston. And in 2006, with staff and board members, we started a fellowship program to prepare people of color for positions in philanthropy. All were considered successful, but the work and the need for further diversity in these professional roles remain.

In some cases, the mission has transitioned into a new work purpose under a different name. The effort to sustain projects like these is tremendous. People change or move on to other positions. Most of the time, the effort was successful.

Now, I commit to give to and support Black organizations and businesses whenever possible. The plan is to identify a few organizations to donate to and provide whatever assistance I can in advisory or technical support. Many of these entities will be small and have limited resources. These organizations provide valuable services to those in need but cannot meet the high demand.

When that time arrives, I will be ready. Pam and I have spent hours thinking about what might happen to our daughter if something suddenly happens to us. Each year, we send her a letter listing our current possessions and where to find things. We offer advice on who to contact and where to seek help if needed. She has asked us, "How do you learn these things?" I'm not sure how you gain this knowledge other than trial and error. No one gives you a lesson. You go through the experience. You heard it said many times, "If I only knew then what I know now." Besides the usual legal documents, we have written a "final wishes" letter that outlines what we want for a service. One of the songs I specify was by jazz pianist Geri Allen, called *Well Done*. The lyrics reflect how I want to be remembered.

Well Done

Long as I will see
My brothers are in need
Lord, let my voice and song touch their souls.
Let my life speak to the heart
Let me share with them how far
You went to show the real meaning of love

(Chorus)
Lord, I pray in all I may win some

Lord, if only one
Let your will be done
There's no happiness in me
If I have not pleased You

When you call my name
I want to hear You say, well done, well done
When I see You face to face
I want to hear you say, well done, well done

These steps help minimize the stress for a family member later and make it possible for us to enjoy the rest of our days knowing the estate, as it may be, is in order. We fully expect a transition that is not so sudden and recognize that much could change between now and then.

Pam and I learned how important this kind of thinking was as we began to have family members depart from us. As we entered the Fourth Quarter, it was very apparent that we concern ourselves with the health of other elderly family members. Often, a family member did not talk with their children or share a legal will, if one existed. As a result, assumptions are made that things will be taken care of or have plenty of time to put this together. Others had wrong or inadequate information about how an estate is resolved or think they don't need to go through a court because the funds are too little. It's not always about money. You may want to decide what happens instead of them leaving it to the courts. From a photo, piece of jewelry, furniture, or china set, to art, or a gift you want to leave to a specific person, there are always mementos. After having a few of these experiences, you understand the need to be prepared as much as possible to ease the transition and be ready for the unexpected.

I could not have imagined the place and space where I find myself today. There is so much for which to be thankful. I start by expressing how wonderful my marriage has been to an exceptional person. Now I am dependent on Pam's support. We have shared lots of laughter and joy. Together we have built a comfortable life filled with memorable experiences. I have had a varied but exciting professional life rich with numerous accomplishments. By the time the Fourth Quarter began, I had started to narrow my scope to a retirement target date. At the time, I did not realize I would continue working in two more exciting jobs before that date. I knew, however, I wanted to teach at a college, but I could not have imagined it would be at Boston College. Now I'm not teaching as I previously thought.

As for leaving Boston, I knew I would be moving somewhere in the south. I had no idea Charlotte would be the place. I would have thought the location would be along the Atlantic coast. We have made this our new home and love it here. We have pleasantly adjusted to the hotter weather and not having to shovel snow.

Struggling with my declining health has been an unexpected and challenging part of my current journey through life. You understand as you age, you get slower and are unable to do the things you did earlier in life. But incurable health issues slow you down even more and become the focal point of everything. This battle continues, which is why I must *keep on moving.*

In writing this memoir, I'm thinking about writing a blog. I have never done this before, but living in the Fourth Quarter is all about trying something new. The objective is to find positive stories or activities and let others know why I like them and why they should. I need to ignore all the negative messages and latch onto actions to help other people.

The other promise I make is to start writing music again. I have procrastinated long enough. Composing was at the top of my list of activities when I retired. Writing words and music will be therapeutic. Being creative with music will have me use a different part of the brain, which has been dormant for decades. There are many challenges to going down this road, but the reward is worth the time and energy. The Fourth Quarter has brought clarity to my life. Writing this book has helped me live with the present and reflect on my past, bringing it all into perspective.

I maintain my love of puzzles by engaging in three online games daily. Sudoku is the most challenging. You fill in the boxes so that each row and column, nine each, contains all the numbers 1 through 9. The game helps you develop your logical thinking and concentration. SET is a graphic card game that features four elements, a number picture drawn from three shapes, three shadings, and three colors. The third game is Pangram, a word game where you identify as many words as you can using only the seven letters displayed in a honeycomb lattice. I enjoy the success of completion and a sense of accomplishment. Pam and I need to play more backgammon, dominoes, and other two-person games, not only for brain exercise but for entertainment. I grew up, like most children, playing board and card games such as Bid Whist. I played cards so much in college I should have earned a degree in the subject. As a family, we mostly play UNO® today.

Of course, I will work harder to get in a bit of exercise regularly. Just walking a little, using the recumbent bike, and weighs at home. Anything that helps my oxygen airflow, blood circulation, and heart-pumping is good for longevity.

I WILL enjoy the moment, but I don't want to be stagnant at the moment. *"Living in the present moment means no longer worrying about what happened in the past and not fearing what will happen in the future. It means enjoying what's happening now and living for today."* (Joshua Becker)

To do this, I WILL enjoy the day by paying attention to the sights, sounds, smells all around me. I WILL enjoy the triumphs and recognize them from where they come. At the end of each day, I WILL write in my journal the positive thing(s) that happened that day and continue to dream, not knowing if it will lead to something better in the future.

I WILL focus on what's most important. In doing so, I WILL determine what I value the most at this stage of my life and decide on what commitments are essential to make. A key element is to leave plenty of time for myself. Also, I plan to spend time with my family and the friends that most matter to me. Beyond the people closest to me, I must practice goodwill and kindness to all that I can.

Finally, I WILL not dwell on the outcomes.
I've already won the game of life on my journey.

About the Author

Ron Ancrum is an expert in nonprofit management and organizational development. His professional career includes college admissions officer, professor, consultant, nonprofit executive, philanthropist, and jazz musician. Ron is a graduate of the University of Connecticut and UMass McCormack Institute for Public Affairs and IEL Education Policy Institute. He has provided consulting services to more than 50 organizations and has built networking relationships across many levels, from college presidents to community organizers.

Ron has served on numerous boards, been appointed to committees, and was a founding member of several organizations.

Born in Stamford, Connecticut, he lived and worked in Boston, Massachusetts for most of his professional career. He now resides in Charlotte, North Carolina, with his wife.

Acknowledgments

I wish to acknowledge the following persons for their support, friendship, and love:

To Erica Ancrum – my daughter, for editing the first drafts and continued support.

My reviewers – Alan Ingram, Marilyn Anderson-Chase, and Harris Gibson, MD

My mother and sister (Clifford and LaMonde) for their love.

To Hubie Jones, my mentor for life. You have been with me throughout my professional career.

The New Year's Eve Crew – Bob & Donna Gittens, Ralph & Debbie Scott Martin, Joy Rosen & J. W. Carney, Mikel & Tyra Sidberry, and Gerry Howland & Shari Nethersole

The ex-Boston - Charlotteans – Willie & Pam Jones, Juanita & Ken Wade, Valerie & John Caldwell, Jerry & Iris Womack, and Lee and Sheila Shephard.

To my various doctors and medical staff – I appreciate all that you do to keep me moving.

CPSIA information can be obtained
at www.ICGtesting.com
Printed in the USA
BVHW031510091121
621183BV00001B/111

9 781953 307804